FOR THE WORLD

Transforming the World Through Deeds of Kindness

andlelights
for the igh School

STUDENT'S WORLD

99 Stories that Touch Lives and Lift Spirits
Written by the Students of
Coral Reef Senior High School
Miami, Florida

Compiled and Edited by Award-Winning Author
Alice Johnson
with Ana Mederos-Blanco,
Theatre Arts Director

Mal-Jonal Productions, Inc.
16713 SW 107th Place
Miami, Florida, 33157-2965

Printed in the United States of America

Library of Congress Cataloging-in-Publication Data
Johnson, Alice and John
Candlelights for the High School Student's World:
Transforming the World Through Deeds of Kindness

ISBN 0-9715032-0-9

Miami-Dade County Department of Cultural Affairs

"With the support of the Miami-Dade County Department of Cultural Affairs
and the Cultural Affairs Council, the Miami-Dade County Mayor and the Board
of County Commissioners."

$\mathscr{C}$ontents

v

$\mathcal{A}$ Message from the Mayor

As Mayor, and on behalf of the over two million residents of Miami-Dade County, it gives me great pleasure to extend heartfelt congratulations to Coral Reef Senior High School's young authors whose essays illustrate a mature understanding of the importance of people helping people.

As father of two young boys I know that young people usually have the best ideas of ways to improve our quality of life and make the world a better place.

I congratulate each of you who contributed to this book. Kindness benefits the giver as well as the recipient. In the wake of the tragedy of September 11, these stories help us understand that beyond the reckless cruelty that changed our lives, there continues to be compassion and caring in our world.

Sincerely,

Alex Penelas, Mayor
Miami-Dade County

ix

$\mathcal{A}$cknowledgments

The things that count most cannot be counted.
—*NEA Journal*

In the compilation of this book, we are tempted to repeat in our acknowledgments the entire index of Coral Reef Senior High School's young authors because, were it not for them whose stories constitute this book as a result of the terrorists' attacks of September 11, 2001, there would not be one.

We thank each of you from Coral Reef Senior High School (CRSH) for your outstanding contributions in making this book a joyful and spiritual reality.

In addition there are a number of people, named and unnamed, to whom acknowledgments are due.

To my kind, compassionate husband, John, who is a victim of severe multiple sclerosis...a disease of the central nervous system that robs motor skills...I express my sincere thanks for the idea of initiating a "kindness curriculum" that would give students an opportunity to express their gratitude through creative writing. To talk show hostess Oprah Winfrey who shared with her ardent listeners, my husband and me, the joy of writing gratitude journals, we are forever grateful.

We are grateful to the Miami-Dade County Public Schools, Miami-Dade County Department of Cultural Affairs, Dade Community Foundations and First Union National Bank of Florida for their deeds of kindness in making this publication possible. We extend many, many thanks to Janell Walden Agyeman, Norma Spector, Christie Ewell, Ana Mederos-Blanco, Edith B. Oden, Delores Washington, and to our graphic artists John Penney, Erika Jacoby and staff for making this dream a reality.

$\mathcal{A}$ Message from the Teacher

As teachers, we know that the test of education is conduct.
In teaching, values always come first.
—*Ana Mederos-Blanco*

As a performing arts teacher at Coral Reef Senior High School, I am fully aware of the responsibility to teach children that values always come first. When I was asked to participate in *The Candlelights Series*, I embraced the project because it teaches values based on the Miami-Dade County School Curriculum. This was also a great opportunity for our students at CRSH to participate in the war against terrorism by using their creative talents in a project drawn from the experiences initiated by the 9/11 event..." Candlelights of kindness for the world."

As an educator of young people, it is my profound belief that the test of education is conduct. It is our responsibility to teach children to want to do their part in helping to transform the world through deeds of kindness.

Based on their everyday experiences, children are aware that the world needs kindness. And because "we are the world" and "we are the children," we have the responsibility of making the world a happier place in which to live by transforming it through deeds of kindness. It is indeed among our responsibilities as teachers to help children become aware of this aesthetic value.

Through multimedia, and especially the events of the 9/11 terrorists' attacks, we learn that the world is unkind only for the lack of kindness of the people who live in it. We can understand the real meaning of kindness by focusing on those human experiences in our lives that project the virtues of kindness. Using this media of personal experiences, the students can clearly see from their writings that kindness is the only kind of praise that is always and everywhere true. When we are kind, especially in our homes, schools and communities, we put others in the place of ourselves.

In addition, kindness also means coming to the rescue of others when they need help, if it is in our power to assist them. Here at CRSH, we have a volunteer program called *Fill the Void* in which our students participate to help the needy through deeds of kindness. I am honored to say that many of my performing arts students participate in the program.

Kindness in the spirit of love is the act of creation and the constant preservation of the world in existence. From divine kindness flow the powers and blessings of all created kindness. This insight is well illustrated in the "Candlelight stories" written by our young authors of CRSH who are sharing with us their wisdom that: (1) The essence of life is love, (2) Love finds expression through kindness and concern, and (3) Kindness is love in action.

—Ana Mederos-Blanco, Theatre Arts Director
Coral Reef Senior High School

*T*his book is dedicated to
the students, parents, teachers, administration, staff
and community of Coral Reef Senior High School.
Thank you all for the many deeds of kindness
you have done for us.
You have shown us that kindness is love in action
and that we can help transform the world
through deeds of kindness.

*"A*nd she (Ann Landers)
was convinced that if any one thing could
serve as a solution to all manner of problems,
it was kindness."

Margo Howard,
daughter of the late Ann Landers,
International Columnist

$\mathcal{I}$ntroduction

Wherever there is a human being,
there is an opportunity for kindness. —Seneca

Children are great teachers. When we listen attentively to their thoughts and feelings, especially following the terrorists' attacks of September 11, 2001, they innocently teach us by examples that the tragedy of life is not death but what we let die within us. They teach us that we humans should learn to FEEL the spirit of LOVE and KINDNESS within us; learn to feel the HAPPINESS within us; render others happy and proclaim our joy! And because we humans are social beings, we should never deny ourselves the JOY of loving others if we are to live together here on planet earth.

As former school teachers who have enjoyed working with children, my husband John and I have learned from them that the beauty and essence of life is kindness. Reflecting on the beauty and innocence of childhood, he suggested that we draw from our caregiver/MS patient experiences and initiate a "Kindness Curriculum." In his passion for imparting knowledge, he suggested that we extend an invitation to children to participate in this "kindness curriculum" by submitting their true stories reflecting deeds of kindness that touch lives and lift spirits. I acceded to his request and our idea has taken form as *The Candlelights Series*.

Because Coral Reef Senior High School is in our community and its performing arts department has presented several of John's and my musical docudramas, I approached Mrs. Ana Mederos-Blanco, the director, with the "Kindness Curriculum" idea. The curriculum, based upon life-affirming ideas so often called upon following the 9/11 terrorists' attacks, would consist of nine chapters containing eleven stories each. The nine chapters would highlight the nine virtues, namely:

(1) Love, (3) Joy, (3) Peace, (4) Patience, (5) Kindness, (6) Goodness, (7) Faithfulness, (8) Gentleness and (9) Self-Control. Because "kindness" encompasses all the virtues, we decided to focus on kindness, highlighting the motif: *Transforming the world through deeds of kindness.* Utilizing this approach, we found *The Miami-Dade County Instructional Objectives for a Balanced Curriculum* to be most helpful.

Mrs. Mederos-Blanco, after discussing the project with Visual and Performing Arts Academy Lead Teacher Mrs. Marta Davis, and receiving her approval, decided that she would participate and the students would receive grade points for their stories. Thus, the project began and would be the first in *The Candlelights Series* of a projected fifty books.

The young authors' *Candlelights Stories* are astounding! While reading and editing many of them, we could not help but shed tears—tears of joy, sorrow, compassion, enlightenment, awakening and for all the beauty of the human spirit. The stories reveal that the essence of life is love, and that writing about our thoughts and feelings is indeed a rich form of meditation, awakening us to transcendent wisdom and universal compassion. The stories enable us to reflect on our own lives, to see the innocent and happy child within each of us. When we adults use this reflection on a daily basis, it enables us to listen to the voices of all children, learn from their thoughts and feelings, see ourselves in them and let their experiences teach us that love is, indeed, a mystery to be lived.

Because children are our future, it is most important that we listen attentively to them with love, respect and appreciation. Children are, indeed, great teachers because they enable us as adults to see the results of our own teachings. Our teachings are reflected in their behavior.

The myriad of children's *Candlelights Stories* compiled in this volume shows us through human experiences that kindness is love in action, and that through deeds of kindness we can help transform the world.

Alice W. Johnson, Ed.D.
Co-Founder/Author, *The Candlelights Series*

PART 1

Candlelights that Touch Lives and Lift Spirits

Written by the Students of
Coral Reef Senior High School
Miami, Florida

*Encourage every child in the development
of his spiritual life, but avoid dogma.*
—*The National Education Association Journal*

SECTION ONE

Candlelights of Kindness and Love

Meet The Authors
L to R - Row 1: Ashley Roberts, Sara Sugimoto,
Loren Beer. Row 2: Dominique Elie, Ashlyn Williams,
Erica Naess, Crissy Izaguirre. Row 3: Meadow Spisak,
Kristina Mirabeau-Beale, Miguel Nolla.
Row 4: Tiffanie Blanco.

KINDNESS: A SYMBOL OF LOVE
By Erica Naess

If every day you stop to say a kind word, it will make all the difference in the world to somebody who needs you.
-E. Naess

In high school, everything seems to revolve around social life. Your friends become one of the most significant portions of your life. So what happens if one day you look around and you realize that all of your friends have drifted away from you or you never had any in the first place? The Beatles sang: "Ah, look at all the lonely people. Where do they all come from?" That's a very good question. It seems that there has always been that one guy who eats lunch alone or that solitary girl who sits apart from the rest of the group.

In this case that lonely soul was a girl who, by outward appearance, looked like the ideal. She was always outspoken in class, ready to make a joke at the slightest provocation. She was attractive and had great grades, to boot. It seemed as though she had it all.

However, it became more and more apparent that, to quote Shakespeare, something was "rotten in the state of Denmark." Her smiles were replaced by far-off stares. She grew quiet and reserved. Yet, no one noticed. Or, if they did, they never attempted to do anything about it. Her peers remained terribly passive.

That girl was, of course, yours truly. It got to the point where I could not keep up the perfect-girl charade when inside I was so alone. I felt invisible. Somehow, nobody knew it.

Nobody realized. Then, one day as I sat by myself in class, a guy who had always been considered an outcast of sorts, approached me and asked, "Are you okay?"

Just the fact that he had bothered to notice and ask the question made me feel a million times better. I wasn't invisible, after all and, as I shared with him my grief, I realized the importance of human compassion. So often it is easy to assume that people are feeling fine or that someone else will fix the problem if there is one. Yet, it is the little things that make the biggest difference.

After that, when I saw a girl alone at lunch staring blankly with her sober eyes, I decided that I would talk to her even if I didn't know her. I told her that everything would be all right and that whatever was making her sad would get better. I told her that even if she didn't realize it, there are people who care about her.

Giving is often a selfish thing because of the satisfaction that it brings. I felt good because I knew that this girl was once me. If every day you stop to say a kind word or show someone that you care, although you may not realize it, it will make all the difference in the world to somebody who needs you.

Erica Naess, 18, will be attending the University of Florida in the fall of 2002. There she will study Journalism and Telecommunications for a year before moving to Southern California to pursue a career in the entertainment industry.

A FRIEND IS A MASTERPIECE OF NATURE
By Kristina Mirabeau-Beale

*Sometimes just giving a shoulder to cry on can change
somebody's life. —K. Mirabeau-Beale*

Sometimes you can sit next to people for years and not
know anything about them. That is how one could describe
my relationship with a lot of my classmates. I tend to be a
reserved person and I don't openly discuss problems with
others.

That all changed at the beginning of my junior year of
high school when I learned the true meaning of kindness and
love. I was walking to class with one of my classmates. We
had spoken a few times before, but about nothing serious. As
I made small talk about the weather, she abruptly told me that
she needed to talk to someone, and could only think of me.
She then confided in me that she had been sexually abused
repeatedly by someone in her household. She was concerned
that her grades were suffering because she found it hard to
concentrate on schoolwork.

She wanted to drop out of our magnet high school. I held
her as she cried. I tried to be calm. Here was a girl whom I
had smiled at almost daily, and who had returned the smile. I
had no idea she was enduring such hideous conditions at home.
I explained to her that she should, under no circumstances,
drop out of school. Her education was the only way out, her
only hope of advancing herself. By quitting she would be
hurting herself. I urged her to talk with our counselor. So,
with my arm around her shoulder, we went to the office and I
left her with our counselor. I wanted to be with her, but thought

it best if she told the authorities in private.

I did not see her again for almost two weeks. I wondered what had happened. Was she in a foster home? Was she still in Miami? Sometime later, I saw her coming out of a classroom with all her belongings. She threw her books against the wall and started crying. I ran to her and she sobbed in my arms. She said that the police had come to her house. Timidly, I asked her if things were better. Then she looked at me and smiled through the tears and said, "No, but they will be." Tears came to my eyes when she said this. I looked at her now as the strongest girl I have ever met. She hugged me, then we gathered her belongings and put them together. She said that, regretfully, because of the legal matters, she could not tell me any details of what had happened. I told her my prayers were with her. As I turned to leave, she stopped me with these words:

"Kristina, I want to thank you. You have given me so much hope. You will hold a place in my heart for the rest of my life, and I don't think I can ever thank you enough."

By now I was crying! We hugged again, and she went down the stairwell. I haven't seen her since, but I hope she is doing alright. I will never forget her. Nor will I ever forget the lesson she has taught me. She made me see that sometimes just giving a shoulder to cry on can change somebody's life.

Kristina Mirabeau-Beale is a senior in the International Baccalaureate program. She serves as the editor-in-chief of a newspaper she created as a sophomore and she enjoys theatre arts and journalism, as well as life sciences. She looks forward to attending Harvard University next year.

STARTING IN THE MIDDLE
By Loren Beer

*In the spirit of kindness and love, it never hurts to say,
"I'm sorry." —L. Beer*

Life is hard at any age, but quite possibly the hardest ages are those between thirteen and fourteen when your life turns itself around and you begin to grow. Oftentimes at this age, decisions are made without considering the possible outcomes. When I was thirteen and graduating from eighth grade, I made a decision that would forever change the way I thought about friendships.

There were five of us, Justine, Laura, Kristie, Monica and myself. We were the three musketeers, except there were five of us. Between grades six through eight we had formed an inseparable bond, a bond that we thought would never be marred.

Toward the end of the eighth-grade year, we were rewarded with an eighth-grade dance, a "senior prom" for middle schoolers. As the time of the dance drew close, my friends and I began to speak about possible dates. Being the optimistic people that we were, we listed all of the most popular and hottest guys in all of Arvida Middle School. Dreaming never hurt anyone. Justine then mentioned that she wouldn't mind going with Jake to the dance. Jake Rasnew was one of our close guy friends, so when Justine made her comment it didn't faze me the way it should have. Either way, Jake had a girlfriend at the time; she was in seventh grade. Moreover, only eighth graders were allowed to attend the big event. Therefore Jake was available, so to speak.

It was lunchtime and everyone was in "spill-out." Spill-out was a caged-in area that all of the students went to after they had finished lunch.

"I was wondering if you had a date to the dance," he asked.

"No, I don't," I replied.

"Well, if you want, we can go together. It will be fun. Would you like to?"

"Sure. Would Mary Ann mind?"

"I already asked her and she is fine with it. What do you say?

In my head I felt the harbinger of trouble, but I ignored it and told myself I was being silly. I wasn't sure why, but I knew something was going to happen. Little did I know what was to come. When Justine and Kristie found out I had accepted Jake's proposal, a little war broke out. Soon it became public. Justine was mad with me, as was Kristie. Laura remained neutral while Monica sided with Justine. It was June 4, 1998, the boom had dropped on Arvida Middle School and there was no going back. That June day was the same day as the National Junior Honor Society banquet. I remember pouring my heart out to my friend Sara Sugimoto, in Dr. Miller's office. Jake soon came to comfort me and I cried on his shoulder. I couldn't understand why they were upset. Jake said that everything would be all right and that Justine and Kristie and even Monica would all cool down about this.

At sunset, as darkness loomed over the banquet hall, anxieties rose. Monica and I had gotten our hair done at the same beauty parlor and had talked everything through. My friendship with Monica was restored and I couldn't have been happier. The night was hard, as was the night of the eighth-grade dance. In between the NJHS banquet and the eighth-grade dance I called Kristie to try to talk things through. We spoke, but not much was accomplished. Notes were written back and forth between Justine and myself. I still couldn't understand what I had done that was so terrible. Jake was a friend to both of us, and besides, the guy had a girlfriend! Yes, I am well aware that Justine had mentioned her interest to go with him, but she also mentioned an interest in other guys. I felt like everything was being blown out of proportion.

Next, Kristie and Justine forgave Jake while I was still in the doghouse. I felt cheated and robbed by my best friends. What did I do that was so much worse than what Jake did? Why was it okay to talk to Jake, and not to me? Why was this terrible ordeal happening now, happening at the end of what was to be an era? Middle school.

School ended; I was talking to Justine. All was right between us. She had called me and we talked about everything. Many tears were shed. I don't think either one of us knew what had happened to our friendship, but we knew the fighting was over, and that was the most important thing.

Kristie and I were still not speaking. Our parents were so worried that they were calling each other back and forth on the telephone about this argument, an argument that none of the parents truly understood. Finally, we made up. One of us called the other; we decided we couldn't go on like this. Not only were we affecting our friendship, but we were affecting the relationships among our other best friends. They were in the middle of our argument, and that was not a good position in which to be.

Truly, I don't know why the two of us fought. Justine cannot remember either. It was a collection of different things. We all just kind of got mad and blamed it on the eighth-grade dance incident. But now, three years later, none of that is on any of our minds. What has happened has taught me about myself, and my ability to forgive and forget. I also have learned that in the spirit of kindness and love, it never hurts to say, "I'm sorry." My friendships with Justine and Kristie are exceptional. Justine attends Killian Senior High, and I, Coral Reef Senior High, but we manage to talk about everything that is going on in each other's teenage lives. She is my counselor, my sister, and my best friend. Kristie and I attend the same school and are inseparable. Two peas in a pod, that's us. We do everything together and tell each other all we possibly can. Altogether, Justine, Kristie, and myself are "the three little pigs," "the Three Stooges," the "Huey, Dewey, and Louie" of the high school realm. We are all that is friendship, and all that is togetherness. I love them.

"I really don't think I could even understand what was going though my thirteen-year-old mind at that time. The issues that seemed so dramatic and urgent then have no significance whatsoever in the present." —Justine Karpt

"To be honest, I don't know why we fought, but I know it taught us all something important. A good friendship can withstand the rough spots, the fragile egos and overreactions. I know ours did." — Kristie Soares

Loren Jennifer Beer is a senior in the Visual and Performing Arts magnet program. Most recently, she performed in "Medea" and was the publicity director for the performance as well. Loren dreams of becoming a prominent lawyer and will continue her studies next fall at the University of Florida.

THE HIDDEN POWER OF KINDNESS
By Meadow Spisak

*When dealing with a large opposing power, one should not
underestimate one's own personal strength.* —*M. Spisak*

He stood outside, fighting for his beliefs. For him, life
revolved around the world being set straight; for everything
to be right, fair and, most of all, unbiased regardless of what
species you were. He was an avid animal-rights activist, who
cared deeply for animals and stood up for them since they
were unable to protect themselves. His goal was to get Burger
King to stop the cruelty done to the animals while they were
being farmed and then also to get them to change the inhumane
way they were being killed. The public and Burger King
were just not listening.

"But what about the animals?" he would say as people
approached the restaurant. He would reach into the depths of
his animal loving soul and tell as many people as possible
about the terrible evils Burger King was committing by the
thousands every single day. Every day he would go to Burger
King, stand outside and talk to people. He would inform
them of what they were endorsing by buying Burger King
products. When he got no great response from the people he
encountered there, he began passing out flyers at his school,
on the side of the road; and he then went to a local news
station. He and others from other animal-rights groups around
the world joined together in fighting the way Burger King
was treating animals.

He helped organize many campaigns against the treatment
of animals, and after several months Burger King announced

that they were changing the way they treated the animals they use to make food, and they were also changing the way in which the animals were slaughtered. By bringing a single person's idea out into the open and sharing it with many people he was able to get other people to take a stand on a very tough issue. The knowledge spread because of this one boy, whose name I never knew, was astounding. He was a candlelight of kindness and love. This shows that when dealing with a large opposing power one should not underestimate one's own personal strength. There is always the possibility that you might reach out and touch the right people who feel as strongly as you do.

Meadow Spisak is currently a senior and getting ready for college. She has a family of five and knows the true value of kindness in people. She cares greatly about all the activists who undertake campaigns that show positive attitudes, and she wishes everyone the best of luck for their lives.

PROUD MUSLIM WOMAN
By Miguel Nolla

In spite of the anger running through all that is "Red, White, and Blue," we must learn to love and to be kind to one another. -M. Nolla

I know a Muslim woman. She is young. She is looking forward to going to college, she is bright, she doesn't wear a veil, and she is not a terrorist.

One of the initial thoughts I experienced after the September 11, 2001, tragedy was of sorrow for all those Muslim Americans who would absorb the shock waves of hate. Sure enough, you saw it in the news: Men who "looked Muslim"; women with veils. Everyone had to wonder about the fear that these Americans must have felt when they saw their own people turn against them because of a slightly different dressing custom, a language, or a faith.

I was sitting in my government class at school and we were discussing Middle Eastern politics. The Muslin woman sat in the class. She looked like she had lost sleep, as had so many other Americans. All of a sudden, out of "Palestinian this and Jihad that" someone asked the kind Muslim woman, "Aren't you a Muslim?" Now, what I expected was a solid "Yes." Actually, I knew this woman. She loved her faith, she was ashamed of no one, she was not even Arabic or Asian for that matter. So, if she survived her parents, surely she would survive a class of peers. Everyone knew the answer she should have given. She said, "No." She left it at that ... "No."

Now I was puzzled. Everyone around her was puzzled but they moved on; I didn't. I had to find out why it was that this proud Muslim woman had all of a sudden denied her faith. At the same time, I was wondering why, I wondered because it was blatant.

I confronted her, impersonally online. She said, "Of course I'm Muslim," and something in the nature of, "In times like these, it isn't something one screams out."

And there it was. In America, Americans made another American afraid of who she is. She is Muslim and American. Our country is one that is a caustic environment for kindness and compassion.

In spite of the anger running through all that is "Red, White, and Blue," we must learn to love and to be kind to one another. Without love and kindness, we alienate the world and ourselves. Without love and kindness, we are not Americans.

Miguel Nolla is a senior who participates in the Legal Academy. During his high school years, Miguel has performed both on stage and in Mock Trial courts. In the future he hopes to pursue some of the creative arts, and he plans to study theatre and film on the college level in the fall.

CANDLELIGHTS OF GRATITUDE
By Sara Sugimoto

Thanksgiving is about love and respect and a special bond of kindness that we all share. -S. Sugimoto

There are infinite aspects of life to be thankful for, yet most people become blind to the things in life that do not directly affect their isolated cocoons. Whether due to sheer selfishness, a lack of knowledge, or simple oversight, we tend to tune out the important bits and pieces that make up the rest of the world ... the things that make our peaceful freedoms possible ... those things that occur in the shadows of the norm. I had the honored privilege to step into a mysterious world of hope, knowledge, power, compassion, determination, and dedication; a world of people who might include the high-school geek, the social outcast, the president of a billion-dollar organization or a simple neighborhood farmer; a group of people who dedicate their lives, bodies, minds, and dollars to make the world natural, greener, safer, a more just place in which to live.

My Thanksgiving was spent at a charity event, a vegan Thanksgiving dinner held by Earthsave, Green Peace, PEDA and other world peace and animal/human rights organizations. I, too, am a vegetarian, but have never seen this aspect of my diet choice. I gave up eating meat simply because I wanted to test my own willpower. This turkeyless Thanksgiving was not about the lack of animal products in the lives of these people...it was about a different way of interacting with the world in which we live and with the people and animals with whom we share this world. It was about making a difference for the sake of others. It was about love and respect and a special bond that we all share, but only some of us are able to truly discover. A seven-year-old girl spoke of the wonders of the world that we take for granted, and an eighty-year-old man told of his dedication to the betterment of society. Young and old, rich and poor, people from all walks of life gathered to share a common goal.

Sitting in one room, I looked around me, observing some of the most intellectual people in society, and knew, deep in my heart, that not only my faith in the future, but also that of mankind was rejuvenated.

Sara Sugimoto, a senior, will attend the University of Florida next fall and pursue a medical degree. She is presently a student in the Visual and Performing Arts Academy for the magnet theatre program.

FREEDOM
By Crissy Izaguirre

The feeling of inner self-realization is true bliss.
-C. Izaguirre

Ever since I could remember I have always looked up to my older sister: Every accomplishment, every failure, every adventure I analyzed and learned from that relationship. Two years ago when she left for college, I developed a fear of deficiency. It was as if, without her, I wouldn't be able to continue. As the weeks passed by, then the months, I realized that everything was going to be okay. I was growing as a person and I no longer felt the need to hide behind anything or anyone. The world was opened to me and my eyes and heart were no longer blinded by comfort.

To put closure to this experience of inner development, this year I have been given the opportunity to take a theory-of-knowledge course, a requirement in the International Baccalaureate curriculum. This class gives us a chance to pause and reflect on our sources and the dependability of our knowledge. It also gives us a chance to create a habit of critical thinking, which keeps us on our toes. Being an independent thinker has taught me to look at things from different angles and respect many other people's opinions. Many say that "ignorance is bliss," but I beg to differ. Now, I can't understand why people aren't eager to learn more about the world or get a taste of who they are. The feeling of inner self-realization is true bliss, something I agree with mind, body and soul. It is a feeling of kindness and love because you feel as one in the heart of all creation. This class holds great meaning for me because it has helped me to assure myself completely that I am not a shadow but my own person. No longer am I that "chick in its shell," for now that I am out, I will fly until I have reached all parts of the world.

Crissy Izaguirre will be attending Florida International University, enroute to her goal of becoming a pediatrician. A senior in the International Baccalaureate program, she will graduate in the top 20% of her class.

MARIA
By Tiffanie Blanco

She saw life as a gift, a candlelight of kindness and love.
-T. Blanco

"Damn, I'm looking good!" Every day, when we would walk into the girls' bathroom, she would look at herself in the mirror and say those words. Maria was one of the nicest, funniest, and most lovely girls I have ever known, and this is the truth. When she was in middle school, she had long, full, beautiful hair. In eighth grade, Maria was diagnosed with cancer. She underwent chemotherapy and lost all her hair. But later in high school, she was feeling better, and she was proud to be happy, whether or not she had her long straight hair. It hurt me to walk down the halls in school and hear people say, "Is that a boy or girl?" When Maria was asked, "Did you shave your head?" she would answer "Yes," with a smile on her face. She saw life as a gift, a candlelight of kindness and love; and every day was a moment that wasn't worth a hard look, a bad attitude or a fight.

One night in ninth grade I went to a party that my friend was throwing. I was pretty depressed that night over some handsome fellow. When Maria came to the party she grabbed me by my hand and took me over to the table where all the chips and dip were set up. We spent practically the entire night standing in front of the food and chatting. She told me to cheer up, that this was a time to sing and laugh. We made up a "chip dance" and sang all the songs that were played. Anything she would have chosen to do to make me feel better would have worked. It wasn't what she did, it was her personality. Maria, of all people, didn't have to try to make a friend happy (we weren't even that close) who was upset by such a minute thing in life, when she had known real sadness and depression.

The thing with Maria was that, in spite of all she endured so early in life, she always carried a smile. She was no doubt the life of the party, ready with a joke to make people laugh. She definitely lived a wonderful life. No one hated her; in fact, she was loved even by her acquaintances. Maria was the definition of kindness. I don't think I have ever met a person as kind as she always was, even on her worst days.

I feel so lucky to have spent the times I did with her. Maria died the summer going into eleventh grade. At her funeral, her sister took Maria's strength and told us to laugh and smile, because if she were alive she would have wanted it that way. The world lost, but the heavens gained the kindest person I have ever known.

Tiffanie Blanco, a senior, a member of the National Honors Society and enrolled in the International Baccalaureate program, is ranked in the top 20% of her class. She hopes one day to pursue her dream of becoming a professional dancer, and she will attend the University of Florida in the fall of 2002.

MY MOTHER
By Ashlyn Williams

"Kindness anticipates others' needs and wishes."

My mother, like all other mothers, is a very special woman. She has helped raise me and has always tried to be there for me. Lately, I have not been very kind to her and I don't like doing unkind things that make her cry. Even so, she has not ceased being a mother to me.

One thing in particular that stands out in my mind that is special about her is that she could feel that I wasn't doing alright even though I wasn't showing it. One thing that contributed to my emotional instability was the death of my cousin, Bobby, in the year 1999, and the death of my cousin, Nicole, ten months later in the year 2000. Besides that, I don't feel like I really have two friends, so sometimes I'm lonely.

The most important thing Mother asked me was, "Are you okay?" I just told her I was and then she still told me that if I needed someone to talk to besides her she could understand. I still said I was fine and left. But one day at school I felt unbelievably depressed. I knew why, but I didn't feel I could talk to anyone, so I just cried and cried, but didn't let anyone see me. Then, finally, I called Mother and told her that I needed help.

Now, I have an appointment with a counselor and I hope that everything is going to be all right.

Ashlyn Williams was born in Los Angeles, California. She is an active member of the International Thespian Society,

Students Working Against Tobacco (SWAT) and the school swim team. Ashlyn is also a drama student. In her spare time she swims with a private team (Swim Gym), watches television, volunteers at her church and helps at the annual Florida Renaissance Festival in Deerfield Beach, Florida.

THE JOY OF FAMILY
By Dominique Elie

My parents are truthful and they are there for me.
—D. Elie

This past month, I think I discovered my family. They have always lived under the same roof as me, eaten the same meals and gone on the same vacations. But, in a way, I never realized why they were there. Adolescence really makes you forget why you have these people around you. It makes you think you only need yourself and your friends and that someone more than twenty years older than you could not possibly understand the melodrama that is your life. In reality, as much like a cliché as this may sound, your parents know exactly what to do in many situations simply because they have been there before.

I have been the type of child who keeps everything to herself. I sit on my bed with the door closed, brooding or crying when I have a problem, praying that the people who live in my house will not ask me what's wrong. I act as normal as possible, which I've gotten very good at, and wait until I can talk to someone wiser, like the kid with braces that sits behind me in math class. However, two weeks ago I had my first breakup and the kid in my math class wasn't there to help. It was the beginning of a long weekend and one in which the only people to console me were those people I had been seeing for the past seventeen years of my life. It wasn't a situation in which I could "just act normal" either.

I sat on my bed crying softly so that no one could hear me, but I soon realized that all that I was doing was creating a river on my comforter. So, I tiptoed in the middle of the night through the double doors that lead into my parents' bedroom, something I hadn't done since I was six and scared of the monster under my bed. I made space for myself between my mother and father and spilled my heart out in a way I had never done or ever wanted to do before. Then the magical thing happened. They were helpful. They didn't ask questions or preach long sermons; they were truthful and they were there for me. It was exactly what I needed. I spent the weekend relying on my family. My dad told me of the little blond girl in his first- grade class who left and broke his heart and my younger sister was even nice enough not to comment on how I was "milking" the situation to get something out of it.

Now, I look back and think of how much good advice I missed out on before just because of my own stubbornness. Yet, I guess I couldn't call myself a full-fledged teenager if I hadn't gone through this "antifamily" phase. It has actually caused me to appreciate my family more than ever before and has made me realize that my relationship with them can never be superseded by anything else. They are, indeed, candlelights of kindness and love.

Dominique Elie plans to study English and continue her involvement in theatre, when she attends Harvard University in the fall of 2002. She knows she'll keep in close contact with her family. She is presently a senior in the International Baccalaureate program.

FEELING THE PAIN
By Ashley Roberts

Time and time again, I said that I really don't care, that I was immune to pain; that I was tough through and through. That I would survive anyhow. That is how I used to live my life, little to know that it would one day change.

One beautiful March day, I was lounging around watching my favorite sport, NASCAR. Just as my favorite driver, Jeff Gordon, crossed the finish line, winning the race, the phone rang. Figuring it was my friend, Carlos, wanting to discuss the outcome of the race, I eagerly snatched it up, but it wasn't Carlos.

That one phone call brought my perfect world crashing down like an avalanche down a mountain. My world filled with emotions, military dreams, family, NASCAR drivers and Nathan. Nathan, barely nineteen and in the Navy Seals. A friendship I never cherished until it was all lost. A friend who stood by my side through thick and thin. One who never judged anyone, found good in even the worst people and situations. The one who would give anything and everything for his country. The one who would give his life for his country— really did. Nathan believed in giving it all for his country and when the time came, when it mattered the most, he followed through.

All I could think about was Nathan, his smile, his laugh, his words, and how his life came to an abrupt stop at only nineteen. Never again will we ever dance, never again would I be able to run to him when I had a problem or tell him about the race. Never will I hear him tell me that he believed in me or hear him say he was proud of my determination. Never will I hear him say to keep trying, even when I most wanted to quit. I learned a month was a long time, six months was even longer and a year was even longer, but this isn't a year nor is it twenty-five years. This is forever! I learned that forever is the longest time of all. But I will forever remember Nathan for his kind personality.

My nonemotional attitude changed that day and nothing hurt worse. I learned how to cry and how to hurt for one I loved. I learned I did not always have to be tough, stable and in control. I learned I did not have to be a rock.

Time and time again I say that I really do care after all. Perhaps I am not as tough. Maybe I am not as immune to pain as I really would like to be, but I will survive anyhow.

Ashley Roberts is in the tenth grade. Though she is in the drama magnet program and loves it, she will not pursue acting as a career. After high school she plans to enter the United States Army, with hopes of becoming a Green Beret. She also hopes to pursue a career as a NASCAR driver, in her father's footsteps. Ashley also wants to major in psychology in college. She says she never wants to give up "the acting bug," so she wants "to act on the side in community theatre."

SECTION TWO

Candlelights of Kindness and Joy

Meet The Authors
L to R - Row 1: Niyama Ramlall, Nikki Bromberg,
Alysia Powell. Row 2: Alicia Pantoja, Kristie Soares,
Akira Spann, Diana Lora, Rebecca Gottlieb.
Row 3: Julianne Scherker, Chante Washington

WHEN SHE NEVER HAD TIME
By Rebecca Gottlieb

Life is full of amazing opportunities and chances.
-R. Gottlieb

Everyone has heard the expression, "Life is short, enjoy it while you can." It never dawned on me that such a common saying could have such a powerful effect. Life is full of amazing opportunities and chances. However, when the lines and margins on the page of our schedule are jam-packed, it is then when it seems that the sting of your lifetime burns shorter and shorter and the days pass by faster and faster.

One little girl used to plan everything into one day and make herself very busy until she realized:

When she was never home,
When she was riding around in a hurry,
When she stepped on others to get where she was
    going,
When she ignored what others had to say,
When she whined about her boredom,
When she was doing homework up until
    the minute she turned it in,
When she walked around with dark circles
    under her eyes,
When she fell asleep in class three times a week,
When she missed her bus in the morning from trying
    to catch some extra sleep,
When she never had time to walk at a normal pace,
When she never had time to watch television,
When she never had time to comfort her friends,

When she never had time to give someone
    a compliment,
And
When she thought her problems were worse
    than anyone else's.
She forgot.
She forgot about the people who listened
    to her complaints,
She forgot about the goldfish she was supposed
    to feed,
She forgot to thank her grandmother for her
    birthday present,
She forgot about her parents who always had dinner
    at the table,
She forgot about the friend she was supposed to meet
    at the mall,
She forgot about the people who attempted to
    comfort others,
She forgot about the person who lent her lunch money,
She forgot about the capability of people to be kind,
And
She forgot the people who were there for her.

    This little girl began to appreciate and recognize her surroundings. Even though life is short and you can only fit so much into your schedule, there is always a little extra room for a "Thank You" to the people who have been there for you a long time–people who have been candlelights of kindness and joy.

Rebecca Gottlieb is a sophomore drama student who enjoys acting, singing and dancing. Ice skating, skiing and playing the piano are her favorite hobbies. She says she has great passion for performing in shows, such as "The Fantastics." She has also directed one production, "She Loves Me."

AN UNEXPECTED GIFT
By *Julianne Scherker*

I never knew how easy it was not only to make someone else feel good but to make myself feel good by doing a good deed. —J. Scherker

On Christmas morning, my mom and I went to a homeless men's shelter. We were with a group of people who were serving food. I had brought my violin to play a few songs for them and I thought nothing of it. When I passed out food, they were more than grateful because they barely had anything. As I was about to leave, I heard two of the men talking as one said to the other, "This is the best Christmas that I've had in a long time."

I realized from that moment on that it doesn't take that much to make someone else happy. It only took a few hours out of my day to make someone else have one of the best Christmas days of his/her life. I never knew how easy it was not only to make someone else feel good but to make myself feel good by doing a good deed. I will never forget that day because since that day I knew that I could only live by helping other people. It gives me great pleasure to help another person, especially one who is in need. I now know that by doing the simplest act of kindness that may seem like nothing to you means the world to someone else. This is, sometimes, the best gift that someone can not only receive, but also give.

Julianne Scherker, 15, is a freshman in the drama magnet program. She enjoys all aspects of theatre including acting, dancing, singing and technical work. She says, "In my future,

I hope to attend the University of Florida and graduate with a major in education." She would like to become a teacher.

OUR WORLD
By Armand Valdes

When we all love again, everything wrong will cease.
-A. Valdes

Too many things are wrong with our world,
Too much for me to count.
Politics and hatred swirled,
Everything taken into account.

Racism between blacks and whites.
Why must we fight?
No matter who we are, we all have rights.
No one is right.

Lesbian or Gay,
Straight or Bi.
Just another way.
Nothing to hate or pry.

Killing is everywhere,
In schools, in church.
We act like we don't care
But in our hearts the guilt will lurch.

Our society is falling apart,
Like a puzzle where all the pieces don't match.
But if we use our heart
Then things will soon patch.

My solution, then
Is peace.
For when we all love again
Everything wrong will cease.

With candlelights of kindness
And candlelights of joy
We can build a world of peace
For every girl and boy.

Armand Valdes, a Critic's Choice playwright, is a sophomore. His play, "How to Beat Everyone Else in Monopoly," will be performed this summer by the City Theatre. He wants "to thank everyone who is helping the fight against discrimination."

THE BEGGAR
By Alysia Powell

If you have a lot, you should give a lot. -A. Powell

Human beings have a tendency to take things for granted. Often, as you've probably heard before, we don't miss things until they're gone. Taking things for granted is an ugly monster that is regret's sister and grief's cousin. For instance, imagine if you lost your job, house, and family. How would you feel?

Homelessness is a huge problem in the United States of America and in most other countries around the world. If you went to sleep in your warm bed and suddenly woke up in the damp streets, you'd be beyond shocked. You'd start crying, "What happened to me?" You don't realize how easily you could end up homeless or impoverished. That is exactly why everyone should have compassion for those that are less fortunate.

One foggy, cold morning in downtown Miami, Derek was walking down the gum-littered sidewalks, on his usual route to his job at a restaurant.

"I'm broke! How am I going to afford to pay my rent? God, help me. Please, God. I need a miracle!" he thought to himself.

As he was walking and thinking, he saw a homeless man sitting on a fence. The homeless man was wearing several layers of ragged clothing. He had a McDonalds cup in his bony, dirt-stained hand, and he moaned as he stretched it out to Derek.

"Sir, sir! Please! Food!" the man said.

Derek didn't know what to do. Sure, he usually gave his money to the poor. He gave his old canned goods to the food bank. Besides, he was broke. He was a few steps away from ending up like that poor guy. He started to walk past "the bum." Suddenly, his conscience hit him hard. He thought, "Oh, well! Okay, I don't have much money, but he has a whole lot less than I do."

And with a feeling of kindness and compassion, Derek handed his last five-dollar bill to the homeless man. The man smiled at Derek, expressing his gratitude. Derek smiled back, his eyes gleaming as he thought to himself: "Gee whiz, I feel so good! Giving money to the needy is amazing! This poor man will buy some food and will be just a bit better off. I guess if you have a lot, you should give a lot; and if you have little, give a little. What a great and joyful way to express kindness!"

Alysia Powell, fifteen, is a drama student who wants to act on Broadway after completing her college education. Her favorite school subjects are drama and history.

WHEN THERE IS A WILL
By Nikki Bromberg

Kindness makes us strong and courageous. -N. Bromberg

In my drama class, I was asked to create a "candlelights" story about a kind, uplifting event that I had personally experienced. I initially thought: "This is crazy! Nothing miraculous has ever happened to me in my incredibly average life." Then, I began to think about a very close friend of mine who not only brought everlasting joy into my world because of her attitude of kindness and determination, but who showed me the true meaning of hope and never giving up. She was certainly a candlelight of kindness and joy. We learned from her that kindness makes us strong and courageous.

You see, my dear friend, whose name is Sally and who was an athlete, had lost her ability to walk in a horseback-riding accident a few years ago. When I heard the news, I had never felt such devastation in my life! My beautiful, kind-hearted friend Sally was never again going to feel the joys of walking or even the wonderful feeling of water rushing between her toes.

I should have known that when the doctors told Sally that she would never walk again, she...of all people...would beat the odds. Sally was the kind of person who could turn any situation into a positive one and somehow manage to uplift everybody's spirits while doing so! And that is exactly what she did. Throughout the period of excruciating pain, she worked day and night to strengthen her paralyzed legs. No matter how much it hurt, she never gave in and always had the brightest smile on her face. In the end, Sally proved the world wrong just as she knew she would do. And even though Sally hasn't, as yet, worked up enough strength to run the ten-mile marathon as she used to, her mobility is improving every day. She can walk slowly for short periods without any assistance from anyone or a walking aid.

Most importantly, Sally taught us all that no matter what comes your way, you must fight until you cannot fight anymore, and that if your heart truly wants something, you will achieve it. Now, what's more miraculous than that?

Nikki Bromberg is currently a sophomore and an active student in the drama magnet program. She enjoys all aspects of theatre and the performing arts, and she hopes to one day become an actress. For now, Nikki enjoys writing, reading, watching movies "and just being a kid."

A SACRED PLACE
By Diana Lora

*"A kind experience is enough to convey sympathy
to the poor suffering heart, and in one instance,
all is right again."*

This may not be a story of kindness or a story of love, but can rather be considered a story of inspiration and faith; one I want to share so that maybe someone somewhere will take it to heart or at least relate to my experience. I had already believed in God and His existence, but was never really the kind of individual to attend church every Sunday or preach the teachings in the Bible. As a Catholic, I was taught to have God in my heart, mind and spirit; and thus it has always been. Yet, not until my trip to France did I truly believe and practice this sacred rule.

On the trip, I was faced with many difficult and detrimental predicaments due to the fact that I was independent from my parents for the first time and cut off completely from all that was familiar. I, along with a group of students, had embarked on this journey to become that independent; experiencing a new world and culture on our own for the first time. The trip held many obstacles for me. It was almost unbearable, consumed with loneliness, solitude and sadness. I decided to make the best of the situations knowing I would eventually return to that place of comfort, a place called home. Two days before departure for home (which I had awaited with anticipation), I overflowed with such emotions from all the problems between the other students and the chaperones, and reservations being canceled, that I could no longer bear it. I needed a place to be alone and think about all that I had learned and realized.

That Sunday morning, I awoke to the sounds of an old cathedral ten feet away from the student hostel where we were staying. I do not remember getting dressed, nor the food on my plate, yet I remember standing in front of the tall, dark, wooden doors, imprisoned by irons that seemed to tell a million stories. I entered the church to hear the voices of angels singing with all their hearts and humble people kneeling to listen to such sweet voices. I continued to walk toward the kneeling people as if I was called. Kneeling down, I began to pray as I never prayed before, surrendering to whatever it was that brought me to the church—to my church—hoping that everything would get better and that my trip was not a complete disaster. Emotions once again overtook me as I looked up to the tinted glass windows and the arched ceilings. Almost instantly, I began to cry, at first because of the sadness and then because of the relief and new security I felt. The whole experience was like candlelights of kindness and joy.

Whether or not it was a coincidence, as I looked to the ceiling, the light penetrated through the stained windows and a family of birds flew directly overhead. It was then I knew that I had been heard and that I was not alone. My faith became much stronger and more powerful. I walked around the cathedral a while longer, knowing I would never forget this place and time. Amazingly enough, things got better. Problems were solved and I no longer felt alone. It was almost perfect, turning out exactly as I had wanted it.

I returned home with souvenirs, pictures and a new sense of feeling for my faith. Things continued to get better, yet I longed for that peaceful place in which hope and inspiration overcame me. I shall return to France someday. I shall return to that church, that cathedral—to my church.

Diana Lora, eighteen, is on her way to college and a hope-filled future. Inspired by her faith, family and friends she looks forward to new life experiences, such as world travel and study abroad, after she completes her high school career. She thanks her mother, her sister and her best friends as she continues to look for the good in people and have faith that love is the most powerful force one can have.

KINDNESS IS THE PERFECT GIFT
By Akira Spann

Kindness never fails to bring joy. -A. Spann

What a day it was; the sun, glistening against the window, filling the room with joy. Kay sat at her assigned desk, taking notes from her teacher. She figured that the day would be much like all the others. It was the season. This time of year always filled Kay with glee. Besides Halloween, Christmas was her favorite holiday. Classes were going on as usual, with few interruptions in between. Yet, today an interruption with good intentions came forth. Two fellow students entered the room. They had an announcement: the Medical Academy was sponsoring an "Angel Tree."

The Angel Tree is a tree decorated with little angels. Each angel has the name of a needy boy or girl. The way it works is that one would sign up to sponsor a kid. The sponsor then had to present a gift for a child to receive on Christmas Day. Kay decided that she would join in the event. She thought: "Think of all the gifts that I have received throughout the years, imagine not receiving a single gift on Christmas Day. I'm going to do my part in giving to those who are in need." So, with that in mind, she signed up to sponsor a child. She would sponsor a little boy. She did, and the little boy's name was Bryan.

Every night, before she lay her head down to rest, she thought more and more about what Bryan would like for Christmas. The thoughts that she had earlier in the day still plagued her. She started to remember past Christmas holidays of her childhood. Her most favorite part of Christmas, besides having two weeks off from school, was waking up on Christmas Day to find gifts under the tree. A feeling that, probably, Bryan had never experienced. Her gift to him was a box of pieces, that, when assembled, would make a car and robot. She thought about the look on his face when he would experience the feeling of waking up to find a gift for him. Even if it wasn't a dozen gifts, it would be one he would treasure.

The day came when the kids from the Medical Academy were collecting the gifts. Kay sat and waited while they collected gifts from the other students. Then, her turn arrived. She felt a great sense of joy as she placed the gift into their hands. The gifts were all collected and the kids went on to the next room. Kay just sat and thought about how Bryan would feel when he would receive his gift. Kindness never fails to bring joy.

"Another good deed well done," she thought.

Akira Spann will graduate from high school in June 2002. She plans to attend college and study theatre arts. Her hobbies include dance, guitar and voice. She plans a career in the theatre.

TO TOUCH THE MOON
By Niyama Ramlall

Using our imagination, we too can be candlelights of kindness and joy. -N. Ramlall

There was once a boy named Lucien who, in my opinion, was a candlelight of kindness and joy. He grew up in a wealthy home in southern France where he lived a very sheltered life and received the most expensive education that money could buy.

Lucien thus became quite a scholarly character, but he soon came to reject the privileged life he lived and decided to set out into the world at the tender age of twenty-three in search of the wisdom that comes only from experience. Lucien decided that his first destination would be Italy, taking with him only a few changes of clothes, some food and money. Being of a scientific and studious nature, he also decided to bring his magnifying glass. When he arrived, he traveled to the countryside where he wandered through fields of barley and sat beneath great willows scrutinizing plant life and dead insects. In the evening he found an inn in which to sleep and eat.

Walking through the farmlands the next day, he found many an angry sheep. As it turned out, they were simply afraid of strangers, but soon enough, he started talking to them, and they curiously started to gather around their new acquaintance. Before long, a seemingly absent-minded young shepherdess appeared playing a lyre and singing, her crook lying on the ground.

Noticing Lucien, she abruptly stopped singing and

dropped the lyre. "Oh," she said, "Who are you?"

Lucien replied kindly, in his perfect Italian accent that he had acquired through his childhood lessons under the tutelage of Madame Flavie Lochet, "Well, hello there. I am a traveler from France and I will be staying at the inn for a while. My name is Lucien. How do you do?"

"Oh, hello, Lucien," she replied, "I am well, thank you. My name is Luna and these are my sheep. I like sheep, but I much prefer to play the lyre, you know."

"So I see, Luna," he replied. "I myself am a scientist and scholar." Then he removed his spectacles and gave her a compassionate, studious look.

However, she gave him no chance to go on, as she excitedly bubbled, "A scholar, you say? Why, you must know many things! I don't even know how to read!" She gazed at him eagerly and expectantly.

Not quite knowing what to say, Lucien decided simply to be frank, "Yes, I suppose I do know a few things, but I have relinquished book learning for a few lessons from experience. I have led quite a sheltered life until now and I wish to become more acquainted with the ways of the world."

Luna was listening intently and appeared to be rather deep in thought. "Why don't you come have dinner with my family tonight? You don't seem to know anyone around here, and we could introduce you to the neighbors as well."

Lucien, although usually a solitary individual, appreciated the warm gesture and accepted the invitation. Before long, Lucien and Luna became good friends and she taught him how to plant, play the lyre, and bake pies. Lucien, in turn, taught Luna how to speak French and how to read both French and Italian. Lucien and Luna soon fell in love, and five years later, Lucien brought Luna and her family to France. Lucien and Luna were married in France. They had a joyful marriage, except that they were unable to have children. After visiting the doctor and having a series of medical tests performed on each of them, they discovered that Luna had cervical cancer. They were now deeply saddened not only because they could have no children, but also because Luna had a terminal illness. She was immediately taken in by the local hospital, all the while accompanied by Lucien.

"Luna, my love," Lucien said tearfully when they were finally alone, breaking the heavy silence, "You're dying!"

"Oh, dear," she gasped, laughing hysterically through the pain. "That could be a slight problem."

"Luna, listen to me, sweetheart. Calm down. I love you very much. I want to do something for you that will make you very happy. What is the one thing you would like more than anything?"

"Oh, Lucien, you know I only wish to live the rest of my life with you," she cooed lightheartedly, leaning her head against his.

"Really, Luna my love, what would you like to do?" Lucien persisted, fighting back the tears.

"Well," she admitted, "I have always wanted to sail to the moon. Sometimes it dips into the water and I know that if only I were close enough, I could touch it."

"Luna, my love..." he started, but he stopped himself. He knew she was serious about this, but he did not want to break her heart by telling her that no one could ever sail to the moon. He smiled compassionately at her, then softly whispered, "Luna, my love, if you want to sail to the moon, then that's what we'll do."

She smiled into his smile as they embraced, tears of kind joy forming in their eyes.

Later, Lucien removed his wife from the hospital, against medical advice, and he proceeded to sell most of their belongings, while she spent her days painting murals on the walls of their house, collecting seashells, and playing the piano and the lyre. Finally, they had only their house, a few belongings, and the money they gained by selling their property. Lucien spent some of the money on a yacht and put the rest up safely into a Swiss bank account. Then, they happily sailed off into the horizon.

On their way to the moon, they joyfully sailed through the canals of Venice where accordion players frolicked giddily along the sidewalks. They reached the shores of Africa, where they encountered mermaids, and proceeded to sail east until they hit the coast of South America and met the Incas and their babies living peacefully in the mountains of Peru. Luna and Lucien continued on their way, dancing merrily on the yacht as it sailed, when Luna, beaming, suddenly collapsed lifelessly in Lucien's arms. Lucien, inconsolable, sailed back to their home with the walls covered by Luna's paintings. Lucien had Luna's body cremated, and once again set sail, only this time, with her ashes. He opened the vial and a gust of wind carried the ashes up, up, up until they seemed to swirl into a point of light that found its new home right next to the moon.

Imagination is a gift of kindness given us; we can make it a joyful experience, he thought to himself. "And like the moonlight, my precious Luna will always be a candlelight of kindness and joy," he smiled and whispered into peaceful skies. Using our imagination, we too can be candlelights of kindness and joy.

Niyama Ramlall is eighteen years old and currently resides in Miami, Florida, with her mother, father and sister. She shares a room with her two pets, a paper dog and a paper mouse. She will continue her education at the University of Florida in the fall of 2002.

PLANTING THE EVERLASTING SEEDS OF HOPE
By Chante Washington

Children have more need of models than of critics. —NEA

At the age of ten, I was faced with a painful physical and mental struggle that I continue to bear till this very day with the inspirational guidance and kindness of Maya Angelou who wrote the bestseller book, *I Know Why the Caged Bird Sings*. When I was ten, I was devastatingly robbed of my "purity" and deprived of my precious virginity and vital innocence. No longer was I able to seize and embrace the cleanliness of my innocence. When my fresh womb of innocent flesh was violated and exploited, I can remember blood treacherously rushing through my veins, conquering my weakening heart and perforating my deep soul. "Yea, though I walk(ed) through the valley of death," I unfortunately feared evil until God sent me a healing angel by the name of Ms. Maya Angelou who cured me to the depths of my soul and contributed to the strengthening of my heart.

Along with my family, Ms. Angelou planted several seeds of hope and conformity inches deep in my failing garden so I could grow to the phenomenal woman that I am today. Because Ms. Angelou went through the same experience and still prospers, not once do I meditate and sob over milk that someone else spilled. I live to see and feel brighter days. I strive to help others and endeavor to become academically successful. Seeing her accomplishments as a civil rights leader, I escape solitude and seek new challenges.

Chante Washington is a bilingual senior in the International Baccalaureate program. She will be attending the University of South Florida in the fall of 2002, where she will study to fulfill her goal of becoming an obstetrician. In addition to compiling over 3,000 hours of community service, she says she has "inspirationally devoted much of my time to shopping!"

A DIFFERENT KIND OF CHRISTMAS
By Kristie Soares

Sometimes it's the bonds that you have with your family that allow you to move on in difficult times. -K. Soares

One year ago, when my parents lost their business, I honestly thought our newfound economic hardships would ruin my life. I had always been accustomed to material wealth; getting a new pair of shoes every month, going out to restaurants several times a week, impulsive shopping, etc. Even though I could sympathize with those who didn't have money, I certainly couldn't empathize with their situation.

I remember that during Christmas one year ago I had an incredible realization of what was important in my life. Because we didn't have any money, I didn't receive any Christmas gifts from my parents. There were literally no gifts for me under the tree that year. I was so embarrassed that I refused to tell any of my friends. I skirted their questions, avoided discussing my holiday, and pretended it was Christmas as usual. Well, that year when I saw all of the wonderful gifts that my friends had gotten, I was overwhelmingly jealous—at first. However, as time passed, I came to realize that this was the first Christmas that my family had been truly united. Sure we had always been in the past, but this year was unique. With no presents to get in our way, my parents exchanged the love that had led us through our rough times. We gave each other support, and in the end that would last longer than a new pair of shoes ever could.

One year after my parents lost their business, I am the exact opposite of the person I was back then. My financial situation has taught me more than just how to handle my money. It has taught me that sometimes the most important things in life can't be bought. Sometimes it's the bonds that you have with your family that allow you to move on in difficult times.

Kristie Soares is a seventeen-year-old student in Miami, Florida. She is a published poet and an animal-rights activist. In the future, she aspires to study literature and write professionally.

GRATITUDE
By Alicia Pantoja

When we are grateful, we learn that living is a great adventure. -A. Pantoja

During high school, you might think that life seems to be a bit too hard, and you might even wonder why it is that you're here anyway if you know that at some point everything will end. We will all end up dead, and people will remember us for some time; later, they will forget. You might not get to that extreme, but you will still question why it seems that the world revolves around you, or that everything seems to be important at some point. How can one get out of this pressuring state when you do not know why waking up in the morning is necessary? I always asked myself these questions, but I will tell you an anecdote that might help a bit.

I moved to the United States when I was twelve years old and the world was just starting to make sense. I can tell you I had many friends whom I had known ever since I was five years old. I knew the story of their lives, their families, as well as I knew mine; their habits, their ways of thinking. I could even predict their reactions. Then suddenly, I was given two months to say good-bye to them and everything that had surrounded me during my entire short life (which was very long for me) and move to Miami. So, I did just what I had to do, and ended up here in Miami with no friends, a new school to go to, and an empty house. Nothing familiar. And I did what you would expect of a teenager: I hated living here, and I held on to memories and friendships that were hard to maintain due to distance. I could not find myself in this place, and started growing up and realizing that every day I was psychologically farther away from my mother. Realizing this and the fact that I was so far away from everything I loved, made me question why it was necessary that I live, breathe and take the bus to high school every morning. I submerged myself in books, and did nothing else but homework and sleep.

One day in tenth grade, I met Alex, a guy at school who helped me understand when my English teacher spoke too fast and I did not catch the words to answer her questions. Alex was not the type of guy who absolutely loved America, and had no worries but video games, like other guys his age. But, on the other hand, I don't think we truly liked the same things either. In any case, he called me once to help me set up a program on my computer, and from then on we started talking on the phone constantly. (I had abandoned the telephone completely since I believed I was only wasting time by chatting with people about nothingness.) But Alex had this whole theory that he was going to get me to like Miami, and I was going finally to see that it was not so terrible to live here.

"It is not that I love this place," he would tell me, "but that it is not healthy for you to hate it so much. You've got to find something here that makes you happy."

And I did. After his constant attempts to convince me of how nice it could be to live here, I gave up. Every time I went out with my sister, I would try to think of all the incredible things I could do in this city that I could never have done in Caracas because of the social and political situation of the country. Plus, Alex made me realize that the point was not actually liking Miami, but liking any place in which you lived.

"The point," he said, "is to mold the place to you, to look for its little things that you can use to make it your home, and learn from it."

And so, I learned that every place has its own marvelous

little things, and it is just a matter of giving up the sadness and nostalgia about an older place. It's just a matter of opening your mind to new options, new views, and new things to learn from. I discovered other cultures, other peoples, other points of view—like Alex's.

And, I also stopped blaming my mom for the fact that I was living so far away from home, and that everything seemed to go wrong. I had always blamed her for the instability of our relationship. But after accepting that it wasn't so bad to live here in Miami, I started thinking more about why things were so wrong with my mother. Then I realized that I had not put in my two cents, and in order for us to get along, we had to talk, we had to face things and, most importantly, I had to do something about it, not wait for her to take the first step.

Time helped me to understand myself, my mother, and why I live where I do. One should, of course, always question things as well as thoughts and feelings...why we live, why we are who we are. But one should never stay in bed and give up on the world because there is a ton of endeavors waiting for you outside the window—friends like Alex, and places like Miami—when you give them a chance.

When we are grateful, we learn that living is a great adventure, and you should not give up the chance of embarking on it because nothing else will give you such a great feeling of joy. At least, I am very glad I jumped off the boat of nostalgia and sadness and am now swimming in a world full of opportunities.

Alicia Pantoja was born in Caracas, Venezuela, on December 11, 1984. She currently is in her last year of high school and hopes to pursue Latin American Studies in order to help Lain American countries through her writings.

SECTION THREE

$\mathcal{C}$andlelights of Kindness and Peace

Meet The Authors
L to R - Row 1: Bianca DeRousse, Chantelle Martos,
Amanda King, Urvashi Ramlall, Nikki Padilla.
Row 2: Heather Ross, Desiree Betancourt, Jarahn
Williams, Ashley Gardana, Monica Palenzuela.

A LESSON FROM PETER
By Heather Ross

Sometimes you need to see beyond the physical and outward appearance and just go for the soul. -H. Ross

I slumped into the chair at the dinner table in the kitchen and sighed. I grabbed my fork and started on the delicious homemade meal. My sister chattered away to my mother (despite the rice in her jaw), and my brother, Peter, sculpted things out of his own dinner. Peter was soon scolded, so he stopped and switched to talking about his day at pre-K. I listened as he talked about disputes about Sandy and playmates.

"Mommy, today I had lunch with Victoria," he exclaimed.

"Peter has a girlfriend," my sister teased.

"Yeah, she's my girlfriend," Peter agreed.

"She's your school friend, Peter," my mother corrected. "So, did you help her eat today?"

Astounded, I wondered what my mother meant about "help her eat."

"Yes, I feeded her and gave her my apple and she liked it and she started laughing cause she thinks it's really cute."

"Why do you feed her?" I asked curiously.

"Because her hands are too small. So I pick up the food and put it in her mouth," he answered, his innocent eyes dancing in the light

My mother explained that Victoria has a physical disorder: her hands and feet didn't form correctly, which keeps her in the wheelchair and unable to use her hands.

"She's so cute, Mommy. We have to buy some more

apples," Peter interrupted.

That made me think. I mean, a four-year-old possesses a maturity and wisdom I may never know. He is able to see beyond the physical and go up to this little girl and talk and play with her, and even help her out and feed her lunch. I can honestly say that at this age I didn't see myself doing something like that. I'm not a mean or unkind person but in my own fear and ignorance, I would rather keep a distance from that person than reach out to her. I don't see myself or most people I know befriending someone who is different and spending lunch with him/her.

Of course, Peter's only a baby and giving a crippled little girl a little apple and calling her his girlfriend isn't going to make the world stop turning, but it is so simple and loving. It makes you realize that sometimes you need to see beyond the physical and outward appearance and just go for the soul.

Heather Ross is a tenth-grade student and is enrolled in the Drama Academy. She has enjoyed writing short stories ever since she learned how to use a pencil. Currently, she is working on a Christian novel about an angel, which she hopes to complete and publish.

TIME

By Monica Palenzuela

True kindness is like water in that it blesses everything and harms nothing.

As time runs its course, things change. Circumstances grow difficult, times grow more complex, and friendships face many challenges and sometimes just collapse. This is where my story begins.

Going into a new school with people I had never met, I think, was one of the hardest things I have ever had to do. Middle school was a whole world, and I had no choice but to explore it. When I walked into my drama class on the first day of the sixth grade, I didn't know what to expect. I was scared, nervous, and afraid that I wasn't going to make any friends. But as I anxiously, nervously, awaited the bell to begin class, I heard a voice. The voice said, "Hello!" I had to look around at first, and then I found the person to whom the voice was connected. It was a girl, around my age, with light brown hair and blue eyes. "Hello!" she repeated. Then I gathered up the courage to say, "Hi!" With those simple words a seven-year-long friendship was born.

My friend and I stayed close all through middle school, never leaving each other's side, and together we moved on to high school. My first day of high school was a replay of my middle-school experience. But this time, I had someone with me on my first day of drama class. She was there for me the whole day and for the rest of the year, offering me support, encouragement and her friendship. But like everything, things had to change. It wasn't until one day in tenth grade that I realized we weren't the two girls who had introduced themselves to each other on the first day of sixth grade. We were no longer twins, but now distant cousins who rarely talked. This time apart was hard, but we both learned about ourselves and we both grew.

In the eleventh grade, we were once again thrust upon each other by having another drama class together. One day while reading a monologue she had written, tears streamed down her eyes, because something very painful hit home. I had been there with her during this awful experience and I knew how she felt and the pain she was going through. At that moment, I forgot the fact that we hadn't talked in months and that we no longer considered each other "friends" and got up out of my chair and hugged her with all of the pain, happiness and memories that I had in me. At that moment we knew that things were going to be okay. We had a connection, a connection of love that didn't have to be spoken or verified, but one that was forever present no matter how far apart we were. This joyful experience has made our lives candlelights of kindness and peace.

Monica Palenzuela, 17, is a senior and has lived in Miami for fifteen years. She is very involved in the drama program at her school and wishes to continue her study of theatre when she begins undergraduate studies at New York University in the fall of 2002.

UNDERSTANDING THE FAITH OF OTHERS IN HUMANKIND
By Urvashi Ramlall

Kindness helps us to understand and respect each other's faith, race and nationality. —NEA

It was May, which meant that at Coral Reef Senior High School, it was Cancer Awareness Month. Melinda's best friend, Jennifer, had been in charge of organizing support activity. Her idea was to organize a school walk-a-thon that started in the evening and went on till the next morning in order to raise money for cancer research. The students taking part would sleep over at the school in sleeping bags and tents on the field outside, and there would be activities all night long to keep the students entertained. Jennifer was very excited as the night drew nearer, and she knew this would be a memorable event.

Melinda, however, did not share her friend's excitement. She was actually dreading the event, and considered not going. When she told Jennifer this, her friend was incredulous.

"How could you ever think about not being there for me? What if something happens and I need you there with me?" she demanded.

But Melinda was still reluctant. Finally, with enough prodding, she agreed that she would go. For the week that remained before the walk-a-thon, she thought about nothing more than how much she was dreading the evening. Still, she said nothing to Jennifer because she didn't want to upset her.

Finally, the night came. Jennifer was ecstatic; she seemed

as though she could not wait to get to the school. She nearly had to yank her friend out of the house by the hand in order to get her there. When they got there, Jennifer immediately flew about every which way, making sure all of the arrangements had been taken care of. Melinda found a chair away from the crowd and sat there silently, not acknowledging anyone.

So the night began, and people arrived in small crowds until there were approximately forty people present. The entertainment kept everyone lively, and the walking was going well, with proceeds coming in at good amounts. As the evening crept on, Melinda watched the events before her. She was surprised to know that so many people cared to take part. After a while, Jennifer came to see how she was doing. She was startled to see tears in her friend's eyes. She asked, "Melinda, what's wrong? What happened?"

Melinda looked at her and smiled. She replied, "I'm just so happy to see so many caring people here."

"Well, of course they care. Lots of people love to be able to help when they can," Jennifer said.

Melinda considered this for a moment. Then she said, "Jennifer, haven't you ever wondered why I don't mention my sister who died years ago? She died of leukemia." Jennifer was stunned, but Melinda continued. "The disease took her so quickly, my parents barely realized what was happening. They tried to go to different doctors for her, but they would all tell my parents the same thing; that the cancer had spread too much for them to do much about it. My parents refused to give up, and they were convinced that the doctors just didn't care enough to do anything much for my sister. Then one night in the hospital, she just decided it was her time to go. She died. That's the reason I dreaded coming here tonight, Jennifer. I was afraid I would see what my parents saw in those doctors—no one caring enough to make a huge difference. But I see that my parents and I were wrong. People had always cared, and they still care, but they can only do what is in their power."

Both Jennifer and Melinda were crying. "Thank you for teaching me an important lesson on life," Melinda told her friend. And Jennifer knew that she had accomplished so much more that night than she had ever imagined she could.

Urvashi Ramlall is a seventeen-year-old student. She loves theatre arts and lives with her sister. She has no pets. Her favorite things are pictures with moons and stars and poems about Gypsies.

THEY WERE MEANT TO BE
By Jarahn Williams

Kindness, gentleness, respect for the feelings of others, and consideration of their circumstances are the chief qualities of a gentleman or a lady. -Lawrence G. Lovasik

Sincere always knew who the girl of his dreams was, but never admitted to his friends who that special girl was. The friends had an idea, but they thought she would be another girl Sincere was messing with. Sincere was a kind, handsome fellow whom all the girls wanted in their lives, but only the delicate, kind ones were fortunate to have him. He blew through middle school with all the girls wanting him, but when he arrived at high school, the girls tended to "hate" him. His middle-school sweetheart went to the high school he attended, and they both knew that the feelings they had for each other in middle school remained.

Through high school, Sincere was very picky with the girls he chose to be in his life. From ninth grade to the end of high school, he had a "thing" for seniors, and they had a "thing" for him. Sincere was pressured by these girls to do things he didn't want to do. His friends tried to get him to do drugs and disobey the law, but Sincere was stronger than that. When he was troubled with problems like that, he went and talked to his middle-school sweetheart. Her name was Janesha. Sincere and Janesha could talk about anything.

One day Sincere had a problem with his girlfriend, and Janesha was having problems with her boyfriend. Sincere saw Janesha in the morning and told her to meet him in the stairwell at lunch time. The lunch bell rang, and Sincere rushed to the stairwell. Janesha showed up with tears falling slowly down her cheek. Sincere wiped her eyes, and asked her what happened. She didn't say, and he just held her in his arms. They looked each other in the eyes, and their eyes sort of sparkled in the sunlight through the screen. Sincere held her hand and said, "Janesha, ever since middle school, I knew you were the one for me, but I failed to see it. I tried to hide my true feelings about you by fooling around with other girls. But no girl makes me feel the way you make me feel, you are special. When I was with the other girls, I thought about you. Before I go to sleep I think about your quiet attitude of kindness."

"What, Sincere?" Janesha asked, astounded.

Sincere said, "I think I love you. Matter of fact, I know I love you!"

Janesha started to cry; those tears were tears of joy. She looked Sincere in the eyes and told him that she loved him, too. She said she was going to break up with her boyfriend, and Sincere said he as going to break up with his girlfriend.

The lunch bell rang because lunchtime had ended. Sincere and Janesha just sat in the stairwell for the last period of the day. They sat there and Janesha just sat in his arms. No words were said. They cried until school was out and kids came running through the stairwell. Sincere and Janesha got up and walked toward the front of the school. Sincere's boys were out there and they were talking about a girl, and Sincere walked up with his arm around Janesha. Then his home-boy, Jalen, said, "Y'all know y'all in love, so why don't y'all just dump y'all girlfriends and boyfriends and hook up?"

Janesha and Sincere smiled and said, "It's already done!"

Sincere and Janesha walked away, disappearing into the light.

Later that evening, Sincere picked Janesha up and they went to South Beach. Hand in hand, they walked up and down the beach while the water ran through their toes. Sincere and Janesha stayed and watched the sunset. It was the most precious thing anyone could see. Janesha fell asleep in Sincere's arms. He kissed her on the forehead and said, "I guess we were meant to be!"

Jarahn Williams is fascinated with relationships. He is active in theatre arts.

KINDNESS TEACHES A LESSON
By Nikki Padilla

*Discrimination and racism can only be solved through
kindness, not violence. -N. Padilla*

A lot of times people get so caught up in their own world
and forget that there are other people living in this world,
dealing with the same problems. It is funny how, when
someone thinks of the world and life, they see taker and
"takee" and mover and "movee," and this is the way many of
us live our lives today. There is a great cloak over what we
do not see. A lot of things happen in other places of the world
and even in our own backyards that remind us that we are all
people struggling in this world. One such example is about
someone showing kindness to me and my family.

My mom doesn't have a particular liking for a certain
group of Latin Americans. It is strange to me because I
normally see Latin Americans as part of our culture, but for
my mom this is entirely different. However, about six years
ago this changed.

It was Christmas Day in 1995. My brother, sister, mother
and I were driving over to my grandmother's house in Hialeah.
On the way there, the car began to make strange noises and
the engine just died. Cell phones were not as popular then as
they are now and were extremely rare. I was ten years old
and extremely frightened. It was cold and my dad was
working that day, but my mom had no idea what to do. So,
we sat on the side of the road, not really knowing how to get
home or call for help. By some miracle, a car stopped and a
guy offered to help because he noticed my mother had her

children there, and it was Christmas Day. The man admitted he didn't know much about cars but he was kind and polite. He drove us to a pay phone and then he left.

Ironically, he spoke with a very distinct Hispanic accent. The guy who helped us that Christmas Day belonged to a nationality of Latin Americans whom my mom thought were all snobs and extremely arrogant.

My mom has definitely changed her attitude toward casting off an entire group as anything, and it has taught my brother, sister and me a lesson: that discrimination and racism can only be solved through kindness, not violence, because that was the only thing that caused my mother's heart to change. My mom is extremely religious and she later told me that she thought God was trying to teach her the lesson that we are all His children and that, sometimes in our lives, we are all in need of help through deeds of kindness.

Sixteen-year-old Nikki Padilla enjoys reading because it is her favorite subject. She has fun spending quality time with family and friends. Adjusting to a busy schedule, she likes to attend school, church and community programs that promote growth.

TOMMY'S SMILE
By Desiree Betancourt

A smile goes a long way. -D. Betancourt

I look up at my picture-filled wall of memories. There is a lot there to remember. I come across this one picture from four years ago. It's a picture of my friend Tommy and I surrounded with a thick decorative blue frame with a silver background. The picture was taken at a park we had gone to for a picnic with our school friends. Many pictures were taken that day, but that one in particular came out the best. Looking at that picture got me thinking about Tommy. We met in high school and we were good friends. Tommy was loved by basically everyone. I couldn't blame them. He was a wonderful person.

But it was the little things he did that I remember the most. He would sit around playing his bass guitar, strumming to his own beat. His funny shirts, his funky necklaces and bracelets and his cute hats were unique. However, that isn't why everybody loved him. He was always helping people out. For instance, one of our friends, Allison, was really sad one day. Her mom had to leave on business on her birthday after she had promised to take her out somewhere. So, Tommy took Allison to the fair, rode rides with her, took pictures, played games and took her home by curfew!

Another time, our buddy Danny's dad passed away. Danny's dad played music for him a lot and he loved that. So Tommy wrote a song for him and played it on his guitar. Tommy's brother, Jaren, had lost a baseball game once; so to cheer him up Tommy sketched a funny picture of the opposing team all fat and sloppy looking.

Tommy put a smile on everybody's face simply because he was always smiling. Tommy was always great to talk to. He was as much a part of my family as my brother was— he was a brother to me. He got me into the weirdest things: music, movies, clothes, jewelry and my favorite, Hawaiian pizza!

I keep saying was; he was a great friend, he was a kind guy. Tommy was in a car accident in his senior year. I rushed to the hospital to see him. I stayed with him for three hours. He knew I was upset and he asked me not to be. I asked him how he could always be so happy. He told me that you should always smile when you're alive so you know that people will cry when you die. And surely enough, it was true. I guess we all learned something from Tommy. We learned that a smile goes a long way and that you are never alone.

Desiree Betancourt, 16, is a sophomore. She is involved in the performing arts and enjoys everything they have to offer. She intends to pursue the performing arts in the future and work in the field.

YOU NEVER KNOW
By *Amanda Marie King*

*Do something kind for someone some day. You can, maybe,
even save his/her life. -A. King*

I can remember it as if it were yesterday when I was
defending Megan from a bully she had known since fifth
grade. Megan was an intelligent girl with a beautiful smile.
She was a wonderful person and she was very confident.
When this bully came around, her self-esteem dropped
extremely. The bully, Kelly, was an annoying girl who
obviously had some issues to deal with. I defended Megan
for almost three years because she had seemed as if she
couldn't handle the pain; and I knew it.

One day Megan had all of her schoolbooks with her and I
wondered why they weren't in her locker as usual. I said,
"Megan, girl, why are you still carrying those heavy books?"

She replied, "Oh, no reason. You know how some things
don't deserve to be in certain places."

"Do you need any help? I can walk you home and make
sure you're safe," I offered.

"No thanks, I'll be all right as soon as I get home," Megan
said in a sorrowful voice.

She looked a bit suspicious, so I insisted on walking her
home. When we arrived at her home, I asked her if she was
feeling all right.

Megan answered me with a hard headshake. "No!"

We began talking about a lot of issues. I often made her
happy, so she was able to pour out her problems to me. Megan
sighed and softly began to tell me what was going on.

"I think you'll be disappointed in me, but here goes. I was in the main hall of school and Kelly passed me. She pushed me out of the way and said, 'Why don't you die already!' I kept asking myself that same question and there was no logical reason why I was here alive. I took all my books out of my locker so my dad wouldn't have to when I'm gone. If you wouldn't have talked yourself into taking me home, I was going to commit suicide. Just a knife and slice the main artery."

I cried and gave Megan a big hug and kiss. I assured her that I'm always here when she needs me. We talked for a long time and she began feeling much better.

There are many similar stories like mine. A random act of kindness can boost up someone's spirit when they're going through what Megan went through. Do something kind for someone some day. You can, maybe, even save his/her life. You never know.

Amanda Marie King is a fourteen-year-old freshman enrolled in the Drama Academy. She enjoys her family, friends and school, including singing, dancing, acting and participating in the color guard, an afterschool activity. She wants to attend college and major in counseling. She also wants to pursue a career as a singer/actress or director.

TESTING LOVE
By Charity Smith

Kindness teaches us that the self-disciplined
life is the good life.

Have you ever had one of those dreams that you were falling and then you jerk from sleep to consciousness realizing that it was only a dream? Well, my experience was sort of like that, but it wasn't a dream and I wasn't literally falling. I met this guy named Robert about two years ago. He actually is the kindest and sweetest guy I have ever met. Our feelings for each other were really strong, so we decided to make it official. But with all the teen melodrama about pregnancy, of being intimate for the first time, cheating and breakups, having a scratch-free relationship was hard. After a wonderful year together of abstinence, he started being influenced by friends who were pestering him to start a sex life. Then the day I never thought would come, came: the day he asked how I felt about sex. I told him that it could be a huge part of my life and not only guys find it interesting, girls do too. But I put our love to the test. I told him that I wanted to wait, not necessarily for marriage to him, but not now. He said that he would be by my side waiting right with me, and when that day comes it will be because we both agree. Now, we're approaching two and one half years happily together after passing the test of love, and I realize I am falling in love.

Charity Smith, fifteen, enjoys writing stories and poems. Later on, she plans to become a lawyer and to publish her own book by age twenty-five.

A LESSON FROM ANNE FRANK
By Ashley Gardana

After everything, I still think people are good at heart.
-Anne Frank

Anne Frank had the courage to say those words when there was no light at the end of the tunnel for her. She was still hoping for people to show her some kindness.

Now, more than fifty years later, we are lost in the confusion of war. Through it all, we still have to find the good in people. "You may not wait a single moment to improve the world," she said in her book entitled, *The Diary of Anne Frank*, a bestseller and classic.

After the terrorist attacks on September 11, 2001, something amazing happened. We became unified as a people. Now, more than everything, I am proud to be American because we didn't wait a single moment to try to improve the world. We have to take the words of Anne Frank and bring her dreams of improvement of people to life.

Ashley Gardana, fifteen, has only briefly considered what she wants to do with life after graduation...and admits she's still clueless. In the meantime, this lively freshman very much enjoys drama and singing.

FAMILY
By Bianca DeRousse

Kindness stops the torrent of angry passion and takes the bitter sting from feelings of loneliness and loss.

My mom and I were never very close. It was my dad I was always together with and whom I talked to about everything.

Then, one awful day he died. I felt so depressed and alone. For a long time I kept myself away from everyone, even my mother. After a while I realized that my mom was also very depressed and alone. It took me a long time to open up to her and begin to be able to share our pain with each other. It was clear that we both loved my dad because he was a very kind person. We knew that we both would always remember him for his spirit of kindness.

I became very close to my mom. We have stayed that way ever since. We talk with each other all the time, especially about my dad and the joy he bought into our lives. My mom and I really enjoy each other and the love of being a family.

She has been there for me and supported me in all the decisions I have to make— especially decisions I have to make as a high schooler. They have been the right decisions because we discussed them and worked them out together. From now on, our beautiful relationship with each other will always be one of kindness and peace.

Bianca DeRousse is a sophomore. She has two siblings: a younger brother and sister. She hopes to fulfill her dream of becoming a professional actress.

FRIENDSHIP CAN SAVE A LIFE
By Chantelle Martos

You never know how kind someone truly is until
you meet him/her. -C. Martos

There was a boy in school whom nobody liked. No one would ever talk with him because they perceived him as being very annoying.

One day I saw him walking home alone and carrying a load of books. I asked him did he want a ride and he said, "Sure."

I drove him home and while enroute, I discovered that he was actually very kind and ... quite cool. Immediately, we became good friends.

From that day on, and because of his kind attitude, we became closer and closer. We joined the baseball team together and would always go to parties together. On our graduation day, I was stunned when he told me that I saved his life! Very calmly, he informed me that on the day when he was walking home alone and I offered him a ride, he was on his way home to hang himself because he felt so lost and lonely, so unloved and isolated, so disconnected and unimportant. He was going home to commit suicide to end the pain of mental suffering. He said that this is why he was carrying all of his books; he was never again going back to school because he felt unloved by his peers.

I was absolutely speechless when he revealed this chapter of his world to me. But I was even more speechless when he said, "You saved my life, Chantelle, because I knew that if one person like you could be that kind to me, maybe I could actually make more friends by being kind."

Yes, I was shocked because I saved his life and didn't even know it! This miraculous incident made me realize that I can never judge a book by its cover. Never! Why? Because you never know how kind someone truly is until you meet him/her. To know others is to love them. This experience taught me that love is a candlelight of kindness and peace.

Chantelle Martos hopes to pursue a career in the arts.

SECTION FOUR

$\mathcal{C}$andlelights of Kindness...
The Virtue That Embraces All Virtues

Meet The Authors
L to R - Row 1: Jeremy Binstock, Rachelle Galindo,
Yvette Wihl, Monique Parris, Ebonie Battle.
Row 2: Marlene Behmann, Derek Sutta, Christie Martin.
Row 3: Fernando Lamberty, Joseph Hammett.

THE KINDEST SURPRISE
By Marlene Behmann

*"Through deeds of kindness, you can bring new life,
hope and courage."*

Face it. As a teenager growing up in contemporary America, we all vaguely base our perception of reality on what we see on the silver screen; from our ideas and relationships, to basic conversation. The thing is, we never, in our wildest dreams, imagine that things really happen that way—but they do.

While rehearsing at school for a comedy in which I was acting, my arm was badly hurt when it was accidentally kicked during a scene in the show. After five hours in the emergency room and wearing a sling on my arm, I found myself the following Monday in pain and at home. Matthew, the boy whom I had just started dating, used the situation to his great advantage. We had been a "couple" for barely a week by then, when out of the blue I had a visitor at my door on my sick day from school. You see, Matthew decided to use his lunch break from work and surprise me. His visit was indeed a surprise. But the biggest surprise was yet to come. When he was getting ready to leave, he wanted me to come out to his truck. Out of curiosity, I went to his truck. Suddenly, he ducked behind his automobile door and emerged with a four-foot-long box with a giant red ribbon tied around it... "To make you feel better," he said with a soft smile. Inside the box were fourteen long-stemmed roses-pink, white and red! "O-o-o-h, thank you, Matthew!" I said, tears of gratitude forming in my eyes. This was indeed the kindest surprise I'd ever been given!

Marlene Behmann, eighteen, is a senior. She enjoys theatre, food and all the other little pleasures that life can bring. Her family and friends have played an influential part in her life, bringing love, laughter and support.

MY FRIEND, ANGELO
By *Fernando Lamberty*

Kindness is one of nature's best means of making others happy. Thoughts and feelings of gratitude make us kind.
-*Mal-Jonal*

My best friend, Angelo, and I have been friends for as long as I can remember. We have always done everything together, but when we entered high school, everything changed. We actually didn't stop hanging out together or anything, but for some reason his kind attitude deliberately changed. He started hanging out with a new group of friends.

Angelo was always an average student, but now he started flunking all of his classes. He even began talking differently and his clothes changed. For as long as I could, I tried to ignore this new, weird behavior of his. But, finally, I couldn't stand it any longer. One day after school, I asked him what was up with this weird behavior, and he said, "Nothing. Why don't you come with me tonight? Me and my friends are gonna have a little fun!"

I thought about it and said, "Fine. I'll go."

So, I went with him that night. We met up with his friends and left in their car. We then pulled up by another car in a broken-down alley. Pretty soon, the car started shooting at us. Two of Angelo's friends were shot. I was frightened beyond words! Immediately, we sped off, driving as fast as we could.

Suddenly, we heard police sirens and we were stopped by the policemen and ordered to pull over to the side of the road. Terrified with fear, we sped away and minutes later, crashed.

I was knocked unconscious.

When I awoke, I found myself in a hospital and two police officers were standing over me. They kept asking me questions and I finally told them everything. They told me that I was not at fault, and that I could press charges against the driver because the accident shattered my left leg.

Certainly, I could have pressed charges, but I didn't. Yes, I could have pressed charges and made Angelo pay for the damages he had done and, in my revenge, teach him a lesson. But Angelo was my kind friend. No matter how much he had changed, he was still my friend. Bonds like ours don't break easily. He got the message through my act of kindness. He is now in reform school, and appreciates the opportunity to change so that he can become a better, kinder and more responsible person—just as he once was.

Angelo was most grateful that I did not press charges and that, in spite of the weird behavior, I was still his friend.

Fernando Lamberty, fifteen, enjoys acting and playing sports. He says that, after high school, "My dream for the future is to get a degree in theatre and become an actor."

THE WAR ON TERRORISM
By Joseph Hammett

Militarism has never kept the peace. -NEA Journal

I've known my cousin since forever. He has always been one of the kindest relatives I have. Now he is twenty-five years old and is in the Marines helping to fight the war against terrorism. Yes, he is in Afghanistan right now with thousands of other Marines. Like other parents whose children have been called to serve in the armed forces, my aunt and uncle are worried out of their minds. I, too, am worried because we have no idea when he will return home, and in what physical and mental condition.

To show our appreciation and love for him, and to give him moral support, we are forever sending him gifts to share with his crew members. He enjoys spreading kindness.

We will never give up on his safe return from service and will always keep the faith, knowing that he will, some day, return home—to the United States where he belongs.

Joseph Hammett is a freshman in the Visual and Performing Arts Academy. He plans to attend college and major in culinary science.

UNENDING HOPE REWARDED
By B. J. Duncan

Kind action speaks louder than words. It says, "I love you. You make me happy. I am glad to see you!"

There was once a young woman who had everything she ever needed in the world. She lived in a nice big house in a good neighborhood, and worked at a well-paying job. The one thing she lacked that would have made her life complete was a child of her own.

The woman and her husband had tried for many years but were unsuccessful at creating an offspring. Finally, after eight years of trying and praying, the woman became pregnant and nine months later gave birth to a healthy baby boy.

The woman's prayers had been answered. She finally had a child of her own whom she could mold into a fine young man. The woman's life, in essence, was complete.

It was around Christmas time, decorations brightened the streets and each individual house had its own identity from lighting designs. The woman and her husband were decorating the family Christmas tree while the baby was asleep in his crib. The baby's crib was located next to the living-room window, which was always propped open in the winter to let in cool, fresh air.

Unfortunately, while the mother and father decorated the tree, someone snatched the baby from his crib through the open window. By the time the boy's mother and dad discovered their baby's disappearance, the baby was long gone and it was too late.

Over the course of time—twenty years—the parents

searched frantically for their son. During that time, her husband was diagnosed with cancer and would later pass away. This left the woman all alone in her quest for her son. She continued searching for him.

One day, when she had almost given up hope, she heard a knock on the door. It was a hot summer day. When she opened the door, a young man kindly asked her if he could mow her lawn for a little pocket change because he was homeless. She agreed because she felt sorry for him, and there was something in his eyes that gave her a familiar feeling. After he was finished with his labor, the woman invited him in for a glass of water to help soothe his exhaustion. He accepted the offer and came in. They exchanged stories and it became more and more evident that they had known each other.

The woman finally realized that this strange man sitting in her living room was her son. She did not let him know because she did not know how to tell him. Instead, she offered to let him come over each week to work for money and to trade stories.

This occurred for several years, up until the woman's death. After her death, the woman specified in her "last will and testament" that everything she had would go to the young man—her son. He moved in and started a family of his own there.

One day he stumbled on a note intended for him from the woman. The note let the man know that he was her son. She told him the whole story. Once he put two and two together, he realized that it was true.

The son who had returned home raised his family in that same house. With this new understanding, he was able to tell some great, true stories about the house and his past.

B. J. Duncan is very glad to be involved in this publication. Throughout his years in the theatre arts, he has ventured into many aspects of the field–most recently, playwriting. His current projects are the musical "Juice," which will debut in the fall of 2002; and his other musical, "Meatcheck," is about the experiences of a group of teenage boys going through puberty.

ANOTHER DAY
By Christie Martin and Jon Lawrence

I would do
Anything, anything for you.
I won't love
Anyone, anyone but you.
And I will say
"No one else, no one else will do."

You'll never know how much
You mean to me,
We'll never know if we were
Meant to be.

I wait for the next time that we can see each other
Though I know you wish us not to be together.
You told me that nothing lasts forever
But I heard once, you can never say "never."

You're afraid to hurt me
Thinking things could never be.
You're afraid I'd hurt you.
Thinking perhaps we would never do.

But in my dreams I will be with you again
And in my dreams we can be more than friends.
And in my dreams we can break our trend
And in my dreams, we can be more than friends...

That day will come when we're awake
Sitting under that shady tree
Staring into the ashtray grey lake
Just "sweet and sour," you and "melancholy" me.

I'll gently touch your lips
With my fragile finger tips.
You'll push my hand away
And so goes another day...another day.

I'LL BE THERE ALWAYS
By Monique Parris

Kind thoughts give power to words and works.

She hit me. I'm unable to walk, and you're missing prom to be with me. I must be special.

I was standing on the side of the road when she decided to drive around the bus, hitting me and sending me airborne to land in the dirt by the side of the road.

I never asked you to come and see me looking like this, but I guess for you it wasn't too much. I have scars on my face that will be there for the rest of my life. I can't walk and have lashed out at you more than once.

You have no idea how I wish I could take back what I said to you two weeks ago. I was just going through one of my withdrawals, and you happened to be there, and I was a bit annoyed at you watching me sleep. It was then I realized that you were just as scared as I was, and not just a nervous wreck. You were scared of losing me, and I was scared of just losing it.

I was sure that you would not be here today, that you would be at the prom with another girl on your arm, wearing my corsage. But I guess you really are here and I am not dreaming. You always told me you were here for me, but for some reason, I wasn't sure that you would be. Once again you have proven me wrong.

I will be forever in debt to you, for it wasn't for you, I wouldn't have had the will to walk again. Every step I take is for you, and I will forever be indebted to you for your thoughtfulness and kindness.

Monique Parris is a senior and drama major who will be attending Lees-McRae College in North Carolina in the fall of 2002. She has been writing since she was in the second grade. She won the poetry award for her poem, "They'll See," in middle school, and she hasn't stopped writing since. "You write your first draft without your pen or pencil leaving the page. Then you go back and make it sound the way you want it to," she says.

NEVER GIVE UP
By Ebonie Battle

The power of friendship is
one of the greatest powers on Earth. -E. Battle

It was track season again and, between practice and schoolwork, Ivory was swamped. The GMAC track meet was approaching in just two days, and her final exam paper for English was due the day after. On top of all of that, Ivory was internally coping with her parents' divorce.

She was having a successful track season and her coach was pleased with her performances on the track, so when she asked for a day off to finish her paper, the coach had no objections. As she left the locker room that day, however, she was still in low spirits. On the way out, she ran into her friend Odessa who asked Ivory what was wrong. Ivory told her, and Odessa then told her to never give up and to continue to work hard, because her future rewards would be that much greater.

After her pep talk, Ivory felt completely revived. She received an A on her paper and a silver medal at the track meet. The power of friendship is one of the greatest powers on Earth, and she was able to succeed with kind and encouraging words from a great friend.

Ebonie Rose Battle, a senior, was born and raised in Miami, Florida. She will attend Spelman College in Atlanta, Georgia, and enter their premed program in the fall of 2002.

HELPING HER HELP ME
By Rachelle Galindo

You can change the life of one person with a simple hello.
-R. Galindo

I'll never forget that young girl I met.
I saw her drop to the floor, all covered in sweat.
Picking up her books,
Listening to how they criticized her looks.

Her name was Jackie,
She was the new girl everyone said was so tacky.

I saw her in my first-period class
Struggling not to be last. Seeing a picture of myself in the
past......

As I saw her being ignored,
And watched her stare at the board,
I wished I could find something to help her out
So she wasn't so left out.

I couldn't think of anything more
Than her face just looking toward the floor.
And that single teardrop from her face
The type u get when u lose that one big race.

Thinking back to lost memories,
When they used to make fun of me.
Feeling like there was no place to hide,

With no one in whom to confide.
Being all alone,
Crying on the phone.

Looking back,
Only seeing things black.

And the one girl that made me see,
The good things I possessed in me.

So right then and there I knew,
How I could separate from the few.
To be different from the others.

It was so simple and so easy
I am surprised I didn't see

How u can change the life of one person
with a simple hello.
And be considered a great fellow.
I made myself and another person feel better,
And I am happy to have met her.

She's been my best friend ever since.
Together to the end.
A helping hand to lend any person in need.

Rachelle Galindo is a freshman, born under the astrological sign of Leo, who enjoys candlelit dinners. She would like to be a lawyer in the future.

THE GAME
By Derek Sutta

Kindness is the powerful virtue that embraces all virtues.
—Mal-Jonal

It was a perfect sunset. The air was cool and the halogen lights had just begun to shine upon the clay diamond. The "Marlin" baseball team, twelve-to-thirteen-year-olds, was geared up, warmed up and ready to play the first-place "White Sox" team. The home plate was swept as the umpire put his hands up and yelled, "Play ball!" The crowd, mainly composed of parents and siblings, roared, making the players feel like the big leaguers.

The first pitch was thrown. "Strike!" yelled the home-plate umpire. The game continued, with the score remaining tied at 0-0. Throughout the game, the field umpire would talk to the first baseman, making sure he wasn't distracted.

At the bottom of the sixth inning, there was a runner on second, and the clean-up batter was up. Tensions were high, as this could be a scoring run. After receiving two strikes in a row, the batter swung hard at the next pitch and sent it high into the air. The center and left fielders both took off after the ball, while the batter took off for first base, rounding it at full speed. He looked for the ball and instead saw the two boys collide into each other.

Not stopping, he headed for second, his eye on the now motionless boys. His coach was yelling at him to keep running, but he couldn't do it. To the surprise of almost everyone, instead of continuing to third base, he ran into the outfield where the boys were. He checked to see if they were still

breathing, quickly realizing that only the centerfielder was—
the leftfielder was not. He tilted the boy's head back and began
performing CPR on him, breathing into his mouth four times
before the boy started breathing on his own. By that time an
ambulance had been called by the coach as the rest of the
people ran over to check on him.

When the ambulance arrived, the paramedic asked the
crowd about who had performed the CPR on the boy, and the
batter said, a bit fearfully, "I did." The paramedic then
congratulated the boy, saying that he saved the other boy's
life. He also added that if he had hesitated, the leftfielder could
have slipped into a coma.

The two injured players spent a night in the hospital, and
were released the next day. The leftfielder, told of the batter's
deed, was speechless. He contacted the batter, thanking him,
and the two families went to dinner that night as an added
bonus. To this day, the boys—who are now men—remain the
best of friends, bound by a simple act of kindness.

*Derek Sutta is a student in the International Baccalaureate
theatre program at Coral Reef Senior High School.*

THE KINDNESS JOURNAL
By Yvette Wihl

Contrary to what the papers say, there is still some good left in the world. -Y. Wihl

As I walked into class one day, I noticed the day's quote on the board: "Practice random acts of kindness and selfless acts of beauty. —Adair Lara" *This is going to be interesting, I thought.*

"Attention, class," my teacher said. "As usual today, we have journal entries. Take a look at the quote and write for ten minutes on what you think it means." I looked at it again, thinking to myself, *It's so self-explanatory....how do I write for ten minutes on it?*

Ten minutes later, the teacher said, "Okay, class, your time is up." I looked up in disbelief. "What?" I said out loud, "I am not finished." I had gotten so into it that I needed even more time. On that day, our teacher assigned us what she called a "kindness journal." Every day we had to do something kind, but it could not be the same thing. It could be anything— from smiling at a friend in the hallway to buying lunch for the person behind you in line.

At first, the class found it dumb, just another grade to make, but our teacher knew what she was doing, we later realized. With this assignment, she forced us to practice kindness, and made us more conscious of it. I soon found myself looking for opportunities to perform it, not expecting to encounter it directly.

I was driving home one day on the turnpike and pulled up to the toll plaza. The bar was already up and the collector waved me on. Puzzled by this, I looked at the collector with my money still in my hand, and he said, "The car before you paid for the three cars after him." A slow smile crept on my face as I put the money back and mumbled to myself the quote from that first day. It was not that I needed to have my toll paid, but it was put in that person's heart to do something unusual. That act touched me. I never got to thank the person, since he was already long gone by then.

Life in Western society is about everyone fighting to get ahead and not looking to see whom they are stepping on. But as I learned through my kindness journal, it costs you nothing to be kind. It only takes a second to perform it and even without the "thank you," the feeling you get inside is beyond words.

"Practice random acts of kindness and selfless acts of beauty." As our teacher challenged us, I now challenge you to put this quote into action, not just once, but constantly in your life. You will see that, contrary to what the papers say, there is still some good left in the world.

Yvette Wihl has a collection of writings she has produced over the years, but this is one of her first to be published. She believes, "It's so much easier to convey emotions on paper than uttering them."

KINDNESS IS FREE...TAKE ADVANTAGE
By Jeremy Binstock

*Sometimes the smallest things leave the
largest impressions. -J. Binstock*

It was the time of communication between the stressed minds of my fellow students. Just after the 9:35 bell and shortly before the 9:45 bell is when the incident occurred.

As I squeezed by the sharp corner on the north wing of Coral Reef Senior High, I observed one of my classmates having serious trouble carrying an excessive amount of books and other school materials—I was surprised that her back tolerated such a weight. It was then that I knew that I had to engage myself in such a way as to help my friend. I was risking a serious "tardy" by doing so, yet I was determined to help this friend out with her numerous materials.

At first, she declined my help, and I exclaimed, "Why walk on a pile of nails barefoot? Give me some of those books to carry." She still refused my assistance until her back began to give out, and then she had no choice but to agree to my aid.

As I gladly walked down the halls, carrying her things to her next class, I realized how much of an impact I could make by doing such a simple and—to some—ridiculous act of kindness.

Of course this act of kindness may seem absurd, but I believe that no act of kindness, small or otherwise, is ever wasted. I have presented my story somewhat dramatically and with great exaggeration, but my objective is truly sincere. As Johann von Goethe said, "Kindness is the golden chain by which society is bound together."

Too many people are led to believe that their impact on someone is too minimal and therefore not worth the effort. But everyone you meet is fighting a hard battle, and random acts of kindness can and will do wonders. They will go a long way, even when unexpected, and sometimes the smallest things leave the largest impressions.

So ask yourself: if someone were to pay you a dime for every kind word you spoke, and collect a nickel for every unkind one, would you be rich or poor?

Jeremy Binstock is a high schooler who loves to read. He enjoys being in the company of his peers and sharing activities with his family. Although he did not share his bio with us, we know that his "Candlelights" story reveals the wisdom of his world.

SECTION FIVE

*C*andlelights of Kindness and Humility

Meet The Authors
L to R: Row 1: Nicole Edwards, Diana Rairden,
Lauren Mayer, Nianen Yu. Row 2: Elizabeth Gorgas,
Mike Palahach, Monica Valdes, Chanel Carroll,
Nicole Milakovich. Row 3: Jennifer Gonzalez,
Katrina Leitner.

A HUG JUST RIGHT
By Chanel Carroll

Kindness drives gloom and darkness from the soul.
— *Mal-Jonal*

My cousin Michael and I were very close. I would always anticipate the days when he would come over to play or the days when my aunt would take us to the movies. He was four years older than I, but it didn't matter. Whenever we were together we always had fun. And one day that all changed.

I remember that day. Tuesday started out like any other day. I went to school—I was in first grade at the time—and after school the bus dropped me off. I remember my grandfather had come to pick me up at the bus stop, but he didn't say anything to me, we just drove to the apartment in silence. I thought something was wrong, but I paid it no mind.

As I stepped into my apartment, I was surrounded by the many faces of my relatives: grandparents, aunts and my mother. As I walked past my mother's bedroom to go to the living room, I saw my Aunt Shelly lying on the bed crying, being consoled by my grandmother. I went to ask my mother what was the matter.

"Why is everyone sad?" I asked her. My mom sat me on the couch and said, "Chanel, today Michael was killed in a car accident."

I refused to believe it. "This is a joke, right?" I asked her.

"No, Chanel, it's no joke."

I couldn't believe it—my whole world had shattered. I couldn't hold back the tears. I was only in the first grade and had never experienced death or anything, but I was old enough to know that I would never see my cousin again. I was then told that my Uncle Adrian had been in the car too. "Oh, no," I thought. "He's not gone too!?"

"No, he's not dead, Chanel," my mother reassured me. However, she then told me that he was in the hospital with severe injuries as a result of the accident. This gave me some relief, but nothing compared to the loss I felt inside. For the rest of that evening, I was in a daze, trying to understand why, and never reached an answer.

The next morning, I went to school, just like any other day, but it wasn't any other day. On any other day, I would have the comfort of knowing that my cousin was alive and well. This day would be the start of a different kind of day, days that I would live with for the rest of my life.

As we started to say the pledge that morning, I began to cry, no longer holding in the sadness from yesterday afternoon. Everyone was staring at me, because I hadn't told anyone what had happened and so they didn't know why I was crying. All of a sudden, I felt arms around me and they felt like the arms of a mother. I turned to see my teacher, Mrs. Rodriguez, looking at me with her reassuring smile, saying that it would be okay. I was shocked at this, because she didn't even know why I was crying, and she didn't care—all that mattered was that I was hurting and she saw that.

Most people waste too much time trying to find out what is wrong and are not as concerned with just giving someone support, no matter what it is. With that one hug, an act of simple kindness, I knew everything would be okay. It just goes to show how much of an effect you can have on a person by just showing them a little kindness and compassion, with no questions asked.

Chanel Carroll does not say much about herself, but she is a sophomore and a very active member of the Visual and Performing Arts Theatre program. She says that she is "extremely grateful to be a part of this collection of stories."

PAY ATTENTION

By Jennifer Gonzalez

It is sometimes helpful to be reminded of certain things and also to lead others by your example. –*J. Gonzalez*

Sometimes, watching or listening to other people's stories can inspire a person to make better decisions about her own life.

There once was a time when a girl complained about not getting enough holiday presents, and she went on and on about how she was dissatisfied with the number of gifts she received at home. A friend she was relaying this to explained to her that "gifts" were simply items of a material nature that, in the end, did not amount to much, and the fact that she was alive and able to open her gifts with her hands was more important.

"I don't care about that. Normal people don't actually think about those things. They only think about how many gifts they are going to get for the holidays."

"That's not true," the friend protested. "Many people realize how fortunate they are that they have the most important things with them already."

The girl didn't seem to care about what her friend said. Counting her gifts, she said, "Nine so far- one more will make ten."

Her friend decided that she would never listen to her because she was so closed-minded.

A few minutes later, they decided to go outside. Out front there was a neighbor who saw them and came over to speak to them. She had scars on her, as if from a fire. She began telling them her story about the scars and that she got them by saving a person from a burning building. This made the selfish girl feel ashamed, for she had cared for meaningless things, while this woman risked her life, just by doing a kind deed.

"Never take anything for granted," the scarred woman told them. "Live each day as if it were your last."

The girl, whose eyes had been opened, asked her, "What happened to the person you saved?"

"She lived," said the woman, "only because I was the only one who went back in to save her."

The girl was touched by her story, and then realized she had been ridiculous by counting how many gifts she had gotten. She then went to gather all her gifts and donated them to charity.

It is sometimes helpful to be reminded of certain things and also to lead others by your example.

Jennifer Gonzalez is a high schooler who enjoys being with family and friends. Her favorite hobby is reading.

KINDNESS CRUSADE
By Elizabeth Gorgas

Kindness helps us to speak the truth because truth is strong,
brave and beautiful. –Mal-Jonal

In this day and age, it seems completely hopeless to try to find someone for whom to perform an act of kindness. On that rare occasion when a person does act kindly to a fellow person, it is generally accepted with hesitation, or with a wary look and a suspicious thought.

I found this best demonstrated once when I bought a bag of Skittles from the school vending machine. After I bought them, I found I was no longer in the mood for the candy, so, in an attempt to be kind, I wanted to give the bag away for free. It seemed like it would be easy enough to do, since so many people enjoy Skittles; but it soon turned from a simple mission to a crusade of kindness.

The first few people gave innocent enough excuses: "I'm not hungry." "I already ate." "I don't like Skittles." But soon the excuses turned suspicious ("Why do you want to give them away?") and even accusatory ("You did something to them, didn't you?"). After what seemed like an eternity of begging and pleading, I finally found a freshman, short in height and a complete stranger to me, who graciously took the candy off of my hands.

I was in shock. Why did this girl, this foreigner to me, trust my kindness, when all my friends, who had every right to trust me and credit my goodness, did not? I told her of their reluctance, then asked her why she trusted me totally and believed me. She gave a simple reply, but it was one that changed my outlook on others, perhaps forever.

She said, "Give me one reason I shouldn't believe your kindness." And that was all.

Elizabeth Gorgas is a sophomore enrolled in the drama program. An ambitious writer, she has published some of her work on the Internet at: http://www.fanfiction.net/ profile.php?userid=127006.

TEARS OF PAIN
By Diana Lea Rairden

Kindness discovers unsuspected beauties of human character and calls forth a response from all that is best in souls. –Lawrence G. Lovasik

Last year, I had been involved in a pretty long relationship, which had been going on two years—a long time by high-school standards—but it was sinking fast. It was so bad that whenever we got together, we would fight. We just could not make it work, but were afraid to let it go. At the same time, the relationship was getting both verbally and mentally abusive; finally, we called it quits. Today, even now that I am over him, I think that it was the hardest thing I had ever done. A lot of the fighting between us at the time was over my best friend, who was a male. My ex was sure that we were more than "friends," but we hadn't even kissed. I said to him that all we were was friends and that was all we would be.

Several weeks after the breakup, I thought that I could handle it without help, that it would stay inside and not bother me. I felt like I didn't need him now, and didn't want to waste any more tears on him.

It was around five in the afternoon one day after practice, and I was walking home with my best friend. All was fine until I suddenly burst into tears over nothing, something so trivial I cannot recall it now. I reached my car, still crying, and climbed in, ready to speed off even though I was in no shape to do so. My eyes and face were already stinging and burning, and I could barely buckle my seat belt. It seemed as though a part of me had been suddenly ripped away—the sort of pain you wish on no one.

As I sat in my car crying, Kevin, my friend, just held me, not saying a word, just listening to me finally spill out all the pain and hurt from the past. He said that no one deserved to feel the pain I did; that in the end the relationship was far from that important. He then took my keys and said he would drive me home, since I was in no condition to drive.

This was a day I will always remember, not for the pain, but because it was so loving. Kevin had allowed me to let go of the pain and smile openly again, something I had not done in ages. This feeling of being wanted wasn't just some fantasy. Because he held me and took care of me and just loved me, it was a day that I will always cherish. I am glad now that I can have Kevin to hold me, and that he loves me as much as I love him.

Diana Lea Rairden is a senior, and she has been involved in drama programs since the fourth grade. She has always enjoyed writing and directing and says she "has no problem being a leader." Diana will continue on the road to success by attending Florida International University, where she hopes to succeed in the field of psychology.

THE NEIGHBOR
By Monica Valdes

*There is perhaps nothing that counts more in life, and the
memory of which lasts longer than random deeds of
kindness.* —Mal-Jonal

I never liked to look at the house to the right of mine
because it gave off an eerie feeling. Every time I would look
at it I would get scared and chilled. Supposedly, an old man
lived there, but I never saw anyone come in or out, and it
looked like one of those haunted houses from the movies, so
I called it the "Grave House."

For fun, my friends and I would sometimes throw things
at the house, just to see if anyone moved in it, but no one ever
did. However, the worst part was that my bedroom window
faced that house, and every night, when I closed the shades,
the house seemed to be watching and waiting for me.
Sometimes, I would see faint lights flicker, but never saw a
soul.

One hot day in July, I finally saw the old man come out of
the house. He was tall, slightly hunchbacked, with long gray
hair in a ponytail. He wore what looked like hunting gear,
including boots, and was unshaven. He had a silver wrench
in his hand, and went to fix his fence. When he stopped, he
walked back to his front door, then paused, bent down and
picked up an object. With an expressionless face, he looked
over at me staring from my window and saw me before I
could move. In his hand was the ball I had thrown over there
a few days before. I stared back and then moved from my
window, and a few seconds later, I heard his front door close.

A few days later I was playing with my friends in front of my house, near a large tree. We would always climb this tree, seeing who could be the first to reach the top. I practiced when my friends weren't around, so I could always climb it the fastest. I reached the top first and yelled that I had made it. My friends would complain that it wasn't fair, and one even asked me how I did it so fast. When I said luck, they of course didn't believe me, and they began to climb down, while I savored my victory. They tried to get me to follow them, but I wouldn't.

After they called repeatedly for me to come down, or they'd leave, I began climbing down reluctantly. I tripped on a branch, and my shirt caught on another branch before I could fall. My friends ran to get their parents, or anyone, to help me. I heard my shirt ripping, ready to give way, when the man from next door came to my rescue. He ran to the tree just as my shirt tore, and caught me safely. I looked at him, and he didn't seem as mean as I'd thought he'd look.

From then on, we became good friends, and I realized that you can't judge a book by it's cover—you have to read it, for you can find things you didn't expect. My neighbor had become my hero with the kind and selfless act of saving my life.

Monica Valdes loves to write stories and is very excited about having one of her creations published for the first time. A sophomore, she loves the theatre and hopes to pursue an acting career in movies or on Broadway.

A WALK IN THE PARK
By Katrina Leitner

Joy is the reward of being kind to others. There is something intrinsically humble about being kind.
—*Father John Gordon*

I was walking in the cold, lonely forest in Austria, Christmas Eve of 1998, a day I can still recall as clearly as if it were yesterday. I had been walking for nearly an hour in the cold, and though it was dark, it was safe. I was enjoying the evening, as most would on this Eve, when I felt a chill wind of uneasiness, and soon after that I heard a cry, the cry that could only come from a little girl.

I walked closer and closer to the cries, hearing them grow even louder. And then I found the girl, a beautiful, angelic-looking child with bright blue, tear-filled eyes. She saw me and was suddenly fearless, as though I had saved her from some terrible monster. She ran over to me and jumped into my arms, making me feel like some great American hero. I suddenly felt like my life meant something, as if I was born to do this. She looked up at me and said, "Thank you." Those words may not sound like much, but when she said them to me, I felt as though nothing else in my life mattered, and simply responded, "Anytime," and we both smiled.

Soon after, I put her down and we started on the way to her house, and were halfway there when we ran into her brother, whose eyes looked like one who had just been given a pot of gold. He ran to her, picked her up and then looked at me and also said, "Thank you." At that point, no Christmas present could match what I felt.

To me, I changed two lives that night, and I actually felt like life was worth living. I soon said goodbye to them and walked home, a huge smile on my face, one that was not likely to be seen again. It was a once-in-a-lifetime smile that I knew nothing could ever match. That night had made me that happy. That Christmas was the best one of my life, and I would give anything to relive that night one more time. This experience had shown me the beautiful candlelights of kindness and humility.

Katrina Leitner was born on June 4, 1986. She spends most of her free time dancing, and she is in a hip-hop dance club called Cuda Flava. She eventually plans to pursue a dance career and wants to be in a video someday. But her "top goal" is to become a veterinarian.

LITTLE RED RIDING HERO
By *Nicole Edwards*

The teacher's life should make a difference in other lives.
-NEA Journal

When I was in fourth grade, we had a contest to see who could best write, "Little Red Riding Hood," in fifty words. Of course, everyone won this contest, so they had another contest to see who could write the story in twenty-five words. Fewer people won this contest, but still it was too many, and so they had a third contest to write the story in ten words. This time, there were only three winners, including myself; so one final contest was begun, and this time the story had to be written in five words. I knew this was no easy task, but I tried my best. I don't even remember what I wrote, but people said that it was very clever for a nine-year-old. So we turned in our papers and waited impatiently for the next Wednesday to hear who won.

That Wednesday I remember as though it was yesterday. We were practicing our cursive writing for Florida Writes when the judge, Mr. Benton, a fifth-grade teacher, came to our class to tell us the results. His opinion mattered to us, and maybe he even liked our papers enough to tell us personally. When he came in, everyone stopped and stared at him as our teacher walked over to him and then asked the three finalists to come forward: myself, Nicole E.; another girl named Nicole B.; and a boy named Tim. He then announced that Tim had come in third, winning a gift certificate to a computer store, and the class clapped.

When he said Nicole next, he didn't say which one—in

our class, everyone, including the teacher, used our full names. My teacher automatically assumed that he meant me and congratulated me on second place and the other Nicole on winning first. It hadn't crossed my mind to ask whom he meant. I just assumed that my teacher wanted what was best. And when Mr. Benton asked the other Nicole to read it aloud, she said it wasn't her handwriting. It was mine.

And here is the twist—instead of my teacher congratulating me, she told Nicole B. that she had made a mistake and it wasn't mine. Mr. Benton grew a little angry and said to my teacher, "No, it is the other Nicole," and was so proud of me that he hugged me and stood up for me. He could easily have gone along with her, yet he defended me and made me feel better after my self-esteem had taken a blow. My teacher bitterly congratulated me.

It wasn't until I told my mother—and also noticed more— that I knew she didn't like me because I was black. She had assumed that the other Nicole was smarter than I was because she was white and I was black. It wasn't until this experience that I noticed how she seemed to have all the black students in a lower reading group, and even treated us differently. When my mother found out about it, she was angry, but there was little she could do other than switch schools, since there was only one fourth-grade gifted class there and I had been in gifted program since the second grade.

At that age I wasn't thinking about racism, and especially not from my teacher. I had only thought of it as a memory, something that had affected my grandparents and maybe my mother's generation a bit, but not mine. What nine-year-old expects to confront it head on? Mr. Benton helped me to realize that he was standing behind me when he didn't have to; thinking of me before himself and for that I will forever be thankful to him. If he happens to read this or maybe see me, and even remember me, I would tell him, "Thank you for believing me when no one else would. You are a truly kind person, and are my Little Red Riding Hero!"

Nicole Edwards, eighteen, will soon graduate from "the great drama program" at Coral Reef Senior High School. She has been accepted to Florida A&M University for a six-year doctorate program in pharmacology. She would like to thank her family and friends for their constant support.

MY FRIEND JOHN
By Nianen Yu

Some people may be able to live without the love of their fellowmen, but the love of others is the very life of the sick.
—Father Damian

Last summer, about three weeks before school started, I remembered that I needed thirty hours of community service before the end of the summer. So I looked in the phone book and went to a number of places to ask if they would allow me to do my community- service hours, but none of them seemed to interest me. I really wanted to work in a place where I could help the community. A few days later, I'd found the place: Coral Reef Nursing Home. I could not believe how stupid I had been, I was right next to it, and even though I had gone to Coral Reef High School for two years, I had never even thought of it. I didn't waste any more time—that day I went to ask for a community service job and started the same day.

The first few days I found that it was not as interesting as I thought it would be and got a little bored. A nurse then said if I had nothing else to do, I could talk to the older people who lived there. After that, things got a bit better. I got to know more people and many of them seemed to appreciate what I was doing for them, so I was very happy to help others out.

One day I saw him—he was sitting in a wheelchair by the entrance, all by himself with no one to speak to, and looking at everyone else. There was a pencil taped to his fragile, insecure hand and a board on his lap full of letters, numbers and simple words. As I approached him he stared at me, and I smiled. He continued to stare at me as I came near to him and asked, "How are you?" He didn't answer, but instead looked down at the board and moved his hands. At first I thought he was deaf, so I asked him louder this time. He started shaking his hand, using the pencil to tap on the board. I was worried by then, because I thought that I had done something to make him angry. When I looked closer, though, I saw that his pencil pointed to the word "fine" on his board. Thinking it was just a coincidence, I asked him another question, "Have you had lunch yet?" And this time it wasn't a coincidence: he used his pencil and pointed at six words on the board: "You-do-not-have-to-scream." I smiled, then laughed at myself and he returned the smile.

We had a short conversation, and he asked me, "Do-you-play-chess?" He smiled and asked me to take him to his room on the north side, and I saw his name printed there: "John Holman." When we were in his room he told me to place a chessboard on the desk, then open the shoe box. Inside was a chess set, so I set it up and we played for more than two hours. By then I had to leave, so I put everything back and pushed him back to the main room. He used his pencil again and pointed out two more words: "Thank you." I smiled at him and said, "You are welcome, and I will see you tomorrow!"

Every day for the next two weeks before school started, I went to the nursing home to visit him and the others who needed my help. I haven't gone back since school started, but I sometimes wonder, "How is John doing now?"

Nianen Yu is a big video game fan who especially likes driving games. Watching action movies, playing basketball with friends and driving, especially, are his favorite pastimes.

OVERCOMING OBSTACLES
By Mike Palahach

"When thoughtfulness and caring are at the core of one's actions, these are genuine acts of kindness and compassion."

There comes a time in one's life when a certain occurrence makes us think, and we learn to appreciate certain things and/ or the people around us that are part of our lives. This happened in the life of a young woman named Loretta. Loretta had one small child and one on the way, also a girl, and this young family lived well in Nassau, the Bahamas. Her husband lived in Miami, so one day Loretta went to visit him there with the young child in tow.

When they reached Miami, the family was reunited and she was glad to be with her husband again. One day, the father went out after work with some co-workers and, while out, fell from the back of the truck he had been riding in and was struck by another vehicle, instantly killing him. A funeral was held some time later, and not long after, Loretta went into labor and soon Julie-Elizabeth was born.

After her birth, the family was forced to stay in Miami (due to age restrictions for traveling) for six weeks. When they were able, they soon departed from Miami back to Nassau. After a period of time, they went back to their daily lives. Years later, there was some political turmoil, and the result was that the government would no longer allow some non-citizens to stay in the country. One day, some government officials came to Julie-Elizabeth's school, took her from there and informed her mother that the child had to leave the country, since she was not a Bahamian citizen. Young Elizabeth was hurt and felt cheated, since both her mother and elder sister were citizens and she was not. But arrangements were soon made for her to stay with some distant cousins in the States, who promised to take care of her.

The cousins, however, made her their servant and didn't allow her to continue her education, instead forcing her to cook, clean, iron and do numerous other tasks for long hours. She would write her mother back in Nassau, but, as she found out later, none of her letters were ever mailed.

In the midst of this, Elizabeth found a woman at her church who knew her mother back in Nassau, and this friend sometimes cared for her. Eventually, Elizabeth began sneaking her things out of the house and taking them to her friend's place. One night she ran away from her relatives and went to the woman's house where, along with the woman's own children, she was well taken care of.

Much later Elizabeth would get in touch with her mother, and when she did, she asked her, "Why did you leave me?" She knew she had not gotten her letters, but still asked, "Why did you leave me, why didn't you try and find me? Why didn't you come here with me?" Her mother's reply is unknown.

Around this time, Elizabeth met a man named J. C. Harris, who was older than her, but he loved her very much and took very good care of her. Some time later they were married and had three children.

Elizabeth had been continuously visiting her mother in Nassau for some time, and still she asked her, "Why?"—Why had she never come and rescued her, why had she had to go through so much at such a young age and why didn't she have what her elder sister had. She even wondered if her mother liked her, a part of her still looking for that acceptance, that love that is felt between a mother and child. Elizabeth, however, still loved her mother deeply, and in some way knew that her question of "why" had been answered. No matter the true answer, she understood that her mother had done the best she could when she lived with her in the Bahamas, and her mother probably did the best she knew how to do when she arranged for her to live with the American relatives. Thoughtfulness and caring were at the core of her actions, and Elizabeth was grateful for this.

Michael Palahach is an International Baccalaureate diploma candidate. Next year Michael will attend the University of Florida on a full scholarship. He is a member of the varsity boys' soccer and volleyball teams, and he also enjoys extreme sports.

JUST A LITTLE ACT OF KINDNESS
By Lauren Mayer

*"We are no better than the magnitude of our kindness
and compassion."*

It was the day after the end of school, and I was looking forward to nothing more than sleeping, eating, relaxing and occasionally going out with my friends. I wanted to spend the whole summer with them, but how could I if I was too lazy to go to see them? Simple: all of my best friends lived in my neighborhood! Nat lived next door to me, Rikki and Drey lived across the street and both Andy and Trisha lived down the street in opposite directions. We had lived here most of our lives, grown up together, and had always attended the same schools, so we were very close. Sometimes too close, as we tended inadvertently to exclude others from our group.

Since it was the first day of summer break, we had all decided to chill at my house in the two hammocks in my front yard. Nat, Andy and I shared one and Drey and Trisha shared the other—listening to music, reading magazines and just relaxing, enjoying the cool breeze. It was kind of uncomfortable with three to a hammock, so I began to get a bit restless. I got up from the hammock rather quickly, causing both Nat and Andy to spill out of it and laughed when they did.

We all had a good laugh until Andy decided to get the hose lying near the hammock and spray me with water. I screamed and ran away, and when Nat took it from him, I started to thank her, until she began spraying me with it, exacting her revenge. It soon turned into a game of two on two, running into the street with cups full of water. Our summer had definitely gotten off to a fine start.

Our fun was interrupted by the horn of a large moving van. Slightly upset, we moved onto my lawn, waiting for the van and the car behind it to move past. Instead, it pulled into the driveway of the house next to Drey's house, which had been recently sold. We all looked at each other, anxious to see who our new neighbors would be. The car doors opened, and the mother appeared, followed by her daughter, who appeared to be our age.

We already had made up our minds about the girl, and began saying nasty things about her clothes, looks and even personal life, of which we knew nothing, and summed her up as a snob who didn't want to talk to anyone else. We then made a pact to ignore her and walked back to my house, after which my friends went home for the day.

The next day we met at Drey's house to go swimming. The new girl and her mother were in their backyard. Her mother was painting her nails, and after she finished, she came over and introduced herself as Donna, and her daughter's name—the one we labeled as the snob—was Shari. When we heard her name, we barely held in a laugh. Donna asked Shari to introduce herself, and she gave a weak smile and said hello, which we thought was an insult, since we were attempting to be "polite." Donna then invited Shari to join us, and she looked like she wanted to, but Trisha then said we had changed our minds and we all walked into Drey's house.

The look of hurt I saw on Shari's face as I went inside made me feel bad for her. She was the new girl, a feeling I knew all too well. I go to a new camp every summer, with people who have known each other for much longer. My friends aren't there and I feel very self-conscious, just knowing that people are talking about me, but I do eventually end up making friends.

With that realization, I caught up to my friends and told them my feelings, saying how we shouldn't be so rude to her, and then added that I was going back out to talk to her. Andy immediately got angry with me, saying I was breaking our "'pact," and that she's a snob and why would I talk to her? I said that we had no right to judge her and that we didn't even know her. And with that, I went back out to Shari and smiled as best I could, then said, "Hi. I'm Rikki." And I saw the warm look of gratitude on her face when I spoke.

Soon, my friends followed from inside, introducing themselves, and we all went swimming, ending the day with a game of Marco Polo that now included Shari. And now there are three to a hammock all the time.

Lauren Mayer has been acting for as long as she can remember. She is a sophomore in the drama magnet program and hopes to act for "many more years to come." Her other favorite activities are swimming, writing and "just relaxing."

FRANKLIN'S BIRTHDAYS
By Nicole Milakovich

My godfather made me realize that life is a gift.
-N. Milakovich

My godfather, whose name was Franklin, was eighty years old and had diabetes. He was also the kindest, most generous man I have ever known.

He was sixty-eight when I was born, and had, by that time, been living with the disease for twenty-five years, so he already had the routine of taking certain pills and not consuming food that contained sugar. At the time, I was not very close to him, and rarely saw him, even though he was an old family friend. One day, however, when I was about seven, my mother told me that he would be coming to our house here in Florida, all the way from Kentucky to celebrate his seventy-fifth birthday, and his wife, Adelia, would be accompanying him. I loved birthday parties, and even though I didn't even know who these people were, I was looking forward to their arrival with excitement.

The day finally came when they were to come and I met them at the door when they arrived.

"Hello!" I said, a huge smile on my face.

"Well, aren't you the most precious little girl," said Adelia, which made me smile wider.

"I can remember when you were about this big," replied Franklin, indicating my once small size with his hands.

They then came into the house and greeted my parents with hugs. The party was marvelous, with champagne for the adults, gifts, and sugar-free ice cream. During the party, I gave Franklin one of his gifts, saying, "Here you go, Grandpa," and handing it to him. Everyone laughed, because I had assumed that he was grandfather because of his age and at the age of seven, I didn't know any better.

"No, honey, this is not your grandfather," said my mother, correcting me.

"That's all right,' he said. "I can just be her godfather."

So from then on, I just referred to him as my godfather and Adelia as godmother. The titles made me feel like I was somewhat related to them, and I loved that. By the end of the day, I had established a close bond with them and was surprised when they brought out a big gift-wrapped box.

"This is for little Nicole," said Franklin. "If I can get gifts, she should too."

I eagerly grabbed the box and unwrapped it. Inside was a 100-piece puzzle set. I had never done a puzzle before, but I wasn't afraid of the challenge. I said thank you for the gift and put it away in my room.

When the party was over, I said goodbye to them and went to my room, then looked at the puzzle. I didn't feel like doing it at the time, so I put it away in my closet for later.

The next year, they came back down to celebrate his seventy-sixth birthday. He was weaker this year, and although I didn't know it, his health was deteriorating before my eyes. "Hello, Fwanklin," I said as best I could. He gave me a smile and bent over, with much difficulty, to give me a hug, then handed me another gift-wrapped box, and of course, it was a puzzle.

Every year after that, they would come from Kentucky to have a birthday celebration, and every year they would give me a puzzle. I never did the puzzles, but just stacked them in the same place in my closet—I never seemed to find the time to start one. But he still came every year, and I was starting to notice that he didn't seem as energetic as the year before, the diabetes becoming tougher for him to battle; but he still came every year to his parties, really seeming to enjoy them.

When I was twelve years old, he came to celebrate his eightieth birthday. "Hello, Franklin, hello, Adelia," I said as I greeted them at the door. They couldn't believe how much I had grown since they had last seen me, and they were happy to see me, but the party was hard to watch because it was hard for Franklin to do a lot of things, and, as always, the food had to be sugar-free for him. Before the party was over, he handed what would be his last puzzle to me. I said my usual thank you, but I also added, "I love you, Godfather," which surprised me since I hadn't expected to say it. And when they got ready to leave Franklin—who was barely able to walk—came over and hugged me as tight as he could, saying, "I love you too, darling." I felt tears well up in my eyes. This man, who was not even my relative, was so kind and gentle, and it had taken me this long to realize that I loved him with all my heart.

Four months after his eightieth birthday, my mom sadly informed me that he had passed away, his diabetes no longer a fight he could win. When she told me the news, I didn't cry, but went to my closet instead and took out the stack of puzzles I had accumulated over the last five years from Franklin, and started with the first one he'd given me. I did every one, sometimes finishing one in a day. I was too young to go to the funeral, so this was my way of mourning his death. And when the last piece was put into place, a single tear fell from my eye and landed on the puzzle.

I had accepted that Franklin was gone, yet I was so thankful that he was able to become a part of me, because he made me realize that life is a gift. What you get out of it depends on how well you put the pieces of the puzzle together.

Nicole Milakovich, fifteen, is a sophomore and an active student in the Drama Academy who enjoys writing, playing the piano and reading novels in her spare time. In the future,

Nicole plans to become an actress, writer and director in Hollywood, California.

SECTION SIX

$\mathscr{C}$andlelights of Kindness and Goodness

Meet The Authors
L to R - Row 1: Jennifer Garcia, Sandra Cardona,
Roxy Garcia, Yvette Wihl, Gauri Sunkersett.
Row 2: Dannel Escallon, Dhanya Czenstochouski,
Frederico Moratorio, LaToya Bundel.

DAY-ZHA-VOUE
By LaToya M. Bundel

*"Kindness teaches us that the first step in the art
of friendship is to be a friend; then making friends
takes care of itself."*

I remember quite clearly a situation that happened in the month of October that impacted my life as well as the lives of two of my friends, Carin and Shayla, whom I hung out with along with another friend named Hollie.

One afternoon, the four of us were all stuck without a ride home, and Shayla asked Carin to borrow her phone so that she could get us a ride home. "All right," she said, "but Hollie's not riding home with us today. She said she was catching a ride with some girl when I was sitting at lunch with her earlier."

Shayla came back and said that she wasn't able to get in touch with her mom, so we found ourselves waiting after school a bit longer, trying to figure out how we could all get a ride home. That's when we spotted Hollie hanging out with a friend of mine named Brian. I guess we were all kind of wondering why she was still here if she was getting a ride from someone, and I sort of felt a bit jealous toward her hanging out with Brian, acting the way they did towards each other. After all, I had always thought that he and I had a closer relationship, since I'd met him first, but I managed to not take it too serious or get mad at either of them.

Finally, I got tired of waiting and suggested to the others that we walk home, since it was a nice day, and not too windy. We all decided that it was a good idea and walked toward the front of the building, finding that Hollie had already left. As the three of us began walking toward one of the streets that led into an intersection, I got a vision of Brian lying in a car after being in an accident, but I kept it to myself because I found it way too freaky.

As we turned the corner past the school gate, Shayla noticed an accident up ahead. We quickly rushed to see what the problem was, but as we got closer, she also noticed that the person in the driver's seat was Brian. We crossed the street and tried to make our way past the accident, so as not to be in the way of things, and for me it was the right thing to do, since I was still feeling out of it from the vision I'd had earlier about Brian being in an accident. However, I wasn't able to keep to that plan because I found myself trying to look in the car at the person in the passenger's seat, but couldn't see because of the sun shining in my eyes. Shayla, who was behind us, ran up to Carin and me and shouted, "Oh, my God, that's Hollie in that car!"

We both stopped where we were and then turned around. I walked back to get a clearer view of the people inside. Once my eyes caught her body, I froze up as mixed emotions and questions ran through my head. Carin seemed to be going through the same process, because all I saw were tears flooding her eyes, and I began crying myself. I am sure that one of the things that was going through all of our minds was that we had just seen her ten minutes or so before, laughing and having a good time.

I thank the Lord that Carin and I had someone like Shayla around us at a time like that, because it was her that kept us together. She constantly told us to just stop where we were and start praying that Hollie and everyone else in the car would be safe. "Carin, you have your phone, right? Start calling Hollie's parents, or someone, and let them know what's going on."

Carin eventually called her mom and told her what had

happened, and that she couldn't reach any of Hollie's relatives. When she got off the phone, she said, "My mom said everything is going to be fine and for us to head for Toya's house"—that was my house. We started out, but Shayla's mom caught up to us, and drove us the rest of the way to my house. When we got there, all we could do was talk about what had happened. I really did thank the Lord again that we had someone like Shayla around, because what she did was truly an act of kindness. I know that Shayla and Hollie are not the most compatible of people, but that Shayla could only think of positive things to do that would help Hollie and her family—even though in the past I could see that they had times that they couldn't seem to stand each other— now, that amazed and impressed me.

The three of us learned a lot that day. One thing was not to ride with just anyone, even if we felt fine about it, and to make sure that our parents know, at all times, our arrangements for getting home, and with whom.

LaToya M. Bundel was born in Guyana, an English-speaking country in South America. She considers herself the athletic type, although she only runs track. She says it is because she wanted a sport in which people "wouldn't dare go up against" her.

A POEM FOR HIGH SCHOOL
By Alana Williams

To me, high school seemed to be one long dream,
Filled with moments of extreme highs and lows:
Where every single thing is not as it seems,
And every student shivers down to his toes.

As a freshman, high school was big and scary,
Filled with cynical and nasty people.

Sophomore year, of those people I was wary,
No one spoke. It was like it was a temple.

Junior year, things got a little better,
The world seemed smaller than when I was little.

From college, I receive a letter,
Knowing my future scares me a little.

With caps and gowns, the dream comes to an end.
Good memories in my mind will I tend.

Alana Williams, eighteen, notes that she has been "raised by two loving parents" who support her in her dream to be an actress. Currently a senior, she will continue her training at a performing arts school this fall.

ANXIETY RESPONSE
By Yvette Wihl

"Life is about kindness and love for one another."

Questions fill my head
Over and over
I ask myself
Are you right
What if....

Life today is full of decisions
And making the wrong one
Would be like
Two trains colliding at full speed.

I am not perfect
So I can't help
But worry about tomorrow's outcome.
I hope I'm not alone in my feelings.

But a word of advice to all others out there
Who endlessly ponder
What our future holds.

Breathe

And know that God is in control.

Yvette Wihl has a collection of writings she has produced over the years, but this is one of her first published works. She believes, "It's so much easier to convey emotions on paper than uttering them."

GOD'S LITTLE MIRACLE
By *Sandra Cardona*

"The art of awareness is the art of knowing wonder, awe and humility in the face of life's unexplained mysteries."

It all started in the city of Barranquilla, Colombia, where Antonia was a happily married woman with five children whose ages ranged from two to eight years and a newborn baby. One sunny day, she received a phone call from her sister-in-law Marina, who asked her if she could watch her newborn son Jesús while she went to the doctor. Antonia agreed and told Marina to bring him by the house the following day at her convenience.

The next day Antonia, while waiting for Marina and Jesús, became anxious and looked out the front door. To her surprise, she gazed upon a beautiful blonde baby boy wrapped in a blanket and placed in a basket on her front porch. She dashed to the child and looked up and down the road for Marina, but there was no sign of her. Antonia finally brought the basket into the house, and the children gathered around to see the beautiful boy.

As the day progressed, meals were served, diapers changed, spills wiped up and both babies were quite content, napping on and off during the day. As the sun set, Antonia became concerned, the whereabouts of Marina unknown to her. Hours turned to days, days becoming weeks and still there was no sign of Marina.

Antonia's husband Juan—Marina's brother—had left for America months before, so he would have no idea about where Marina would be. She recruited the help of her friends and neighbors to help search for her, but unfortunately, she was not heard from again.

Antonia soon grew to love Jesús as much as one of her own. Juan would often travel back to Colombia from the United States, and he too grew to love Jesús. They had another child the following year, a girl, with the children now numbering seven including Jesús.

At night, she would pray and one night, as she lay awake in bed, she began to think of her own baby boy that she had lost in a tragic accident. He was about the same age as little Jesús was now when he died. She then believed that Jesús was a miracle sent by God. The miracle that mended her broken heart —Jesús was God's little miracle.

Sandra Cardona was born in Baranquilla, Colombia, on November 12, 1984. She plans to attend the premed program at the University of Miami. She is presently enrolled in the International Baccalaureate program. Ultimately, she says, "I would love to become a psychiatrist or an actress."

THE IMPORTANT THINGS OF LIFE
By Jennifer Garcia

*I was rich by just having someone who cared for,
and loved, me.* —J. Garcia

My family was never very wealthy. All my life I envied the girls with the nice clothes, new shoes and the best toys. I never had any of that and so I always thought that I was unlucky and even cursed. Why couldn't I be happy like the rest? Why did the kids in school have to make fun of me for having holes in my jeans, when it was all that I had? Why did the teachers ask me to print my projects when I did not have a computer?

I only had a few toys and one very special doll that was dirty. She had no clothes and patches of hair were missing, but she was my best friend. She was what I cherished the most. I always bragged about having a doll and even though it was not much, I thought it was special because I had a toy like everyone else in school. But one night my house got robbed and everything was either destroyed, broken or missing, including my favorite doll. I cried for weeks afterward. Could things get any worse?

My parents didn't have much money, and I didn't have the heart to ask them for a new doll, so I had to entertain myself by playing with my grandmother, cousins, brothers and sisters, as well as the rest of my family. We played hide-and-go-seek, doctor, teacher and many more games. My tears eventually stopped and soon turned to smiles, and some of the biggest laughs I'd ever had came from my mouth. This was when I realized that material things were not the world.

The better games were the ones that I made up. Pretending to be a princess in the castle that was made out of a cardboard box, with my dog as the dragon, was so much better than a stuffed dragon. Money did not mean a thing. I was rich by just having someone who cared for, and loved, me.

A few years later, my father got a better job and we were a little better off economically. That Christmas, they bought me a new bike, doll, shoes and the prettiest pink shirt I had ever seen. I was happier to be able to share that time with my family than to receive any of those things. From that day forward, I was a different person, and I never again envied the girls with the nice cars or the newest shoes. I just stopped and took a moment to be thankful for everything I had—not for material things, but for a place to live, a family to love and warm food to eat. Because, when you think about it, those are the only things that really matter in the world.

Jennifer Garcia is sixteen and loves to write stories and poems. This is the first piece she has ever submitted for publication.

"LUCK" BEYOND BELIEF
By *Frederico Moratorio*

*In gratitude for your own good fortune you must render in
return some sacrifice of your life for other life.*
-Albert Schweitzer

I never really paid too much attention to the fact that I
had a complete and orderly family until September 11th, when
a stroke of luck came to our family.

A few days before the 11th, my older brother and I were
left home alone because our parents had gone to New York.
It was an ordinary trip and no one had any reason to worry
about anything. They called us every day to tell us how they
were doing. They originally planned to come back September
11th, at around ten o'clock in the morning, then decided that
they wanted to see us before we went to school that day, so
they changed their flight to September 10th, not knowing what
a giant change that would be.

On the tenth, they arrived at 11:30 am and we were all
happy to see each other again. On the eleventh, I went to
school and everything was normal until someone ran into our
classroom and told us to put on the news. We did, and we
saw the tragedy and heard the announcements that all the
airports were closed. I then knew that my parents would not
have been able to come home if they had not changed their
flight time, and my brother and I would have been left without
food or money for an undetermined amount of time.

When I got home, everyone began talking about the good
luck we had.

But that wasn't all. The events of September 11th made

me realize how lucky we had been a month earlier. We had planned a trip to the Grand Canyon. The trip included a helicopter ride over the Grand Canyon. We cancelled the trip due to complications. We later learned that a family of four went on the same company's helicopter on the same day we were to have gone, and they ended up crashing. These two events made me realize that I am very lucky to have my family, and to appreciate them, because we may not have such good luck in the future.

Frederico Moratorio, fifteen, was born in Montevideo, Uruguay, under the astrological sign of Libra and has "a normal family of four." He enjoys long walks on the beach, hours of fun and laughter on the phone.

A HARSH LESSON
By Dhanya Czenstochouski

Seeing things like these (the terrorists' attacks) happen in such a raw, real way helped me come to a harsh realization about how selfish people can really be. -D. Czenstochouski

Today I woke up complaining about the time and how it was too early. I groaned about being tired, and got up to take a shower I thought was way too cold. When I got downstairs for breakfast, I found I had nothing I wanted to eat. I was late to my bus stop, and I argued with my mother. I got to school, saw my friends and went to class to complain about how much work we had to finish. My day was off to another great start.

At the end of what seemed like an eternal first-period history class, we turned on the television to watch our cheesy morning announcements. As we talked and giggled, our attention was suddenly drawn to a horrible sight. A plane had crashed into now smoke-billowing World Trade Center towers, and the announcer was yelling, almost in tears, trying to explain that another plane had crashed into one of the towers just seconds before.

The thought of how many people were in those buildings made me sick. Hearing the story escalate to an attack in three major cities made my heart drop to my stomach and tears well up in my eyes. That could have been one of us—me, my family, my friends—people I don't know and those I see every day. It could have been any one of them.

People die every day. It's nature taking its toll on everyone, just as it was intended to do. But seeing the mass murder of innocent citizens who thought it was just another day at work saddens me worse than anything else I have ever heard. Watching as we mourned this unnecessary loss gave me a sad and empty feeling inside.

A friend of mine cried all day, because her father was on a connecting flight through New York and she couldn't get a hold of him. Seeing things like these happen in such a raw, real way helped me come to a harsh realization about how selfish people can really be.

How selfish are you, to kill so many people who had no right to be killed just for a cause that you believe is righteous? And as for me—who cares how early I have to wake up? At least I can wake up. Nothing in my fridge I like? At least I've got food enough to eat. My mother and our fight? I'm thankful that I have a mother.

Seeing something like this really gives our society a slap in the face. It wakes us up and tells us how selfish and caught up in ourselves we can be. The only way I can deal with this is to turn a negative into a positive. We have to see tragedies like these as a way to take into consideration the things we should appreciate and how many things we take for granted. Behind every misery, there is a reason. And this is reason enough to make what's left of our society better.

Dhanya Czenstochouski, fourteen, is a thespian who enjoys dance as well as drama. She is currently enrolled in the magnet drama program and aspires to become a professional actress.

FROM THE MOUTHS OF BABES
By Gauri Sunkersett

*From this story, I hope we can all remember how innocent
we all were at one point, when someone's skin color,
gender or wealth did not matter. All that mattered was
how the person was on the inside–trusting,
loyal and fun to be around.*

Once upon a time, there was a little boy named Anthony.
Anthony was the youngest of five children. The two eldest
were girls, and the other two siblings were boys. Because
Anthony was the youngest, he often looked up to his brothers
and sisters. One day, Anthony's parents told him that they
would be moving out of their small town and into a big city.
Anthony was excited! He had never been in a big city before!
He endlessly wondered about how tall the buildings would
be, how many cars would be on the streets, and what kind of
stores he would see; but never once did he consider that he
would meet people from around the world in the big city.

Once he got there, Anthony immediately noticed the
difference. Everywhere he went, he saw a mixture of people.
He was used to seeing just one kind of ethnicity, so this
variation excited him. Immediately, he made friends with
people of other cultures. In fact, he even had trouble
pronouncing his new best friend's name. But none of that
mattered to Anthony, for all he was looking for in a person
was someone who was honest, loyal, trusting and fun to be
around.

Unfortunately, Anthony's brothers and sisters were having
a difficult time fitting in. They were not so open to change

and would continually avoid walking by people who looked different from them. So his four siblings had trouble making new friends, and they hated city life. One day, Anthony's eldest sister, Cristina, walked into Anthony's room and saw him playing with his new friend. She felt it was an outrage. She yelled at Anthony so much that his best friend was embarrassed and went home without saying goodbye to Anthony. After this, Anthony was confused. He could not understand why Cristina had yelled at his friend. They were just playing with trucks on the bedroom floor. A kind of game that children of all cultures play. He was completely baffled.

Then Cristina laid it out for him. She told Anthony that his friend was different from them, and that the two different groups should not mingle. Anthony said that was the craziest thing he had ever heard, and ran off to find his true friend.

Gauri Sunkersett is a senior in the International Baccalaureate program who plans to attend the University of Florida on the premedicine track, where she will study to become a cardiovascular surgeon. At the moment, his hobbies include Indian classical dancing, tennis and playing the piano.

REAL FRIENDS ARE FOREVER
By Roxy Garcia

*"A friend is a kind source of refuge and strength to
those who walk in darkness."*

There was once a young girl named Adrienne. She was a
very attractive-looking girl who got good grades, came from
a good family and was very popular. She had many friends,
but there were four who were very special to her. The five
girls had been best friends since kindergarten. They grew up
together and were more like sisters than friends. Anytime
one of them needed something or was in trouble, or just needed
someone to listen to her, she always reached out to the others.

One day, during their freshman year of high school,
Adrienne met Xavier and immediately fell for him. Now, all
of the other girls had boyfriends; but none of those
relationships had ever caused as many problems as this one.
Xavier was a very nice guy, but he didn't get along too well
with Adrienne's friends. So it became hard for Adrienne to
balance the time she would spend with her friends and the
time she spent with her boyfriend.

As the relationship became more serious, Xavier began
demanding even more time from Adrienne, so the time she
spent with her friends became less and less. Eventually, her
friends only saw her when they passed her in the hall. When
they tried to call her, she would immediately make an excuse
to hang up, so that she could go back to talking to Xavier.

This began to bother her friends. They had been together
for so long, but as soon as a guy came into the picture, she
had dropped them quickly. Eventually their group of five

became four. Her friends were very hurt. They never thought this would happen. They had always told each other that they would never pick a guy over each other and would never let one come between them, because their friendship was too strong and too precious to do that. They felt betrayed.

Adrienne was with Xavier for a year and a half before they got into a huge argument and broke up. Since Adrienne didn't talk to her friends any more, she had nowhere to turn. She realized then what she had allowed to happen. She had gotten so totally and completely consumed with Xavier that she was blinded and didn't notice what she was doing. She realized that although she was very popular and had friends, her real friends-the ones who listened to her, helped her and loved her for the real person she was, were no longer there. She felt all alone and horrible about what she had done. She didn't know what to do. She figured her friends would be mad at her and wouldn't want to speak to her. She thought that if she went back to them and tried to talk to them, that they would think that she was using them, because Xavier wasn't there for her any more. She became very sad and depressed.

The following week at school, the moment she walked in, her friends were there waiting for her. As she walked toward them, she didn't know what to think or why they were there. When she finally got to where they were, they immediately told her that they heard about her breakup and wanted to see how she was doing.

Adrienne immediately burst into tears. She knew what she had done to her friends and no matter what, they were still there for her. Before she told them what had happened between her and Xavier, she apologized for everything she had done, and of course they forgave her. From then on, any boyfriend of Adrienne's never came between her and her friends. She would never make the same mistake twice.

Rosanne "Roxy" Garcia is a junior who greatly enjoys dancing and singing. She says she ultimately wants to attend the University of Florida and become a lawyer.

A STRANGLED HEART
By Dannel Escallon

"The gift of kindness is an outgoing,
overflowing way of life."

May 30, 1992, was a joyous and sorrowful day. My brother, Dariviel Jesus, was born–with liver failure. Fear stuck my family in a way I couldn't even explain. My parents spoke to the doctors at the hospital about what was going on. The doctors explained that my brother was born with severe damage to the liver and was not going to make it.

At the time, I was confused. I couldn't understand why someone just beginning to live was going to die. My parents did not accept the doctors' words and fought to see if there was something that could save him. Sure enough, three angels came to save him. These men opposed everything the hospital was saying and stood tall to find a way to save my brother. The names were Dr. Vargas, Dr. Sirlin and Dr. Gonzalez. Dr. Vargas and Dr. Sirlin arranged for him to be transferred to Chicago Children's Hospital where Dr. Gonzalez was waiting to receive him. He was part of the liver transplant team at the Chicago hospital and accepted the case, even though my brother was so critically ill.

Dariviel Jesus was transferred to Chicago at six days old. When he arrived he was so ill that the head of the liver team didn't think he would survive overnight. While waiting for the liver, my brother became even more critically ill. He had blood exchanges and transfusions three to four times a day to keep him from becoming poisoned by the ammonia in his bloodstream. On the eleventh day of his life, my brother went into a coma. One of the doctors wanted to remove him from the transplantation list. But Dr. Gonzalez convinced her to keep him on the list and give him a chance to get a transplant because that was his only hope of survival.

At thirteen days old his liver was transplanted. We all rejoiced, but unfortunately, there was small price to pay. During the waiting period for his new liver, he had several seizures that caused bleeding and destroyed his retinas. Eventually he went blind. That hit us very hard, for he had lost his ability to see, which made him weaker than he was already–or so we thought. A surgical procedure was attempted on both eyes to help him regain his vision, but all failed. He had a very low immune system and was on several medications.

Dariviel Jesus has since overcome many obstacles and is a strong boy. During his first four years of life, he was in and out of the hospital several times with illnesses caught because of his low immune system. But each time he recovered well. He did not walk until the age of five. We were all worried that he might not be able to walk independently, but he kept trying until he finally did it. Now he is nine years old, strong and healthy. He has some development delays, including speaking, but he understands both Spanish and English and can communicate in both. He attends a visually impaired/multi-handicapped class. He has learned to compensate for his blindness by using his other senses to guide him. Life is not easy for him, but every day he grows stronger to face it.

Death came knocking on the door and instead of hiding behind it or just giving in, he fought back and overcame death. It was a hard period in my life. I will never forget it, though, because it was a time when my family stood tall and defied the odds. Today, I am glad that my brother is with us and is a healthy, special little boy, full of life and love to share.

Dannel Escallon was born on August 26, 1984. He is a

senior and participates in the magnet dance program. He also belongs to the Thespians and has received several awards for his costume designs and musical performances. Dannel plans to study film in the near future at New York University.

OUT OF THE DEPTHS
By Stéphanie Delatour

Life is a matter of control and understanding. - S. Delatour

I once heard a story that touched my heart and opened my eyes to a true hope of a better life. My ears and eyes witnessed the painful but proud tale that was the cause of erupted tears of melancholy. This is the story of a girl who lived in agony caused by her drunken father and her mother who cheated constantly on her father. The story took place in Mexico City, my hometown, when the girl was just a teenager. Neither her father nor her mother ever physically abused her; nevertheless, the damage was deeper and more painful. Without even noticing it, she was all alone. The mother was never home. Her father lived in his office with a bottle of whisky.

One afternoon she realized that she was alone with nobody to talk to, nobody to laugh with or even listen to her. She left the coldness of loneliness and touched the thorns of emptiness. The internal pain caused by that was ineffable; the emptiness inside her was killing her.

She waited every day for time to go by as quickly as possible. She watched the hands of the clock go by, one by one, and she listened to the everlasting sound of the ticking. She cried every night in silence, and her throat had become so scratchy that it hurt even more. Her tears were dark and cold and there was no handkerchief to dry them, nor a soft voice to tell her everything was all right. She knew it wasn't. Her days became rainy and the hypocrisy of both her parents had become just another stab in her back. She couldn't deal with it any more. She couldn't say anything because she was muted by fear–fear that haunted her every night.

One day she decided to put an end to her fears and to her life, too. She wanted to commit suicide by getting drunk and swallowing some pills, and to make sure, to drown herself in the pool. Her mother saw her in the pool and jumped in to get her out. She was in a hospital for one month and went to the psychologist every week. But that wasn't much help. She needed something much bigger, she needed her life back, she needed love back. But the worst awaited her.

She became alcoholic, like her father. She then mixed this addiction with drugs and she thought she was happy. But this was the lowest point of her life. She was really drowning in the dark side of life. She was in such bad shape that she couldn't take care of herself and was almost raped. Her parents decided to send her to a rehabilitation center out of the country. She agreed without even knowing what was going on.

So her journey started here. Although she had not been taking drugs for such a long time, she was addicted and that was enough to kill her. So the "hardest" part was to survive three days without alcohol or drugs. She went crazy. She felt like her body was eating itself up, that she couldn't go on any more. But she did, she stayed sober for more than six months and she felt that she didn't need the poison anymore. Everything seemed perfect; she talked often with her parents and learned that her father had quit drinking too. The patients in her treatment center even decided to go on a trip to the beach, which was a couple of hours away. She was happy for the first time, after years of pain.

But her story doesn't end here. The eventual trip back home was wonderful and she had fun as never before. She needed her parents, but she knew that they were fine–well, that's what she thought. On September 19, 1985, her life changed again when Mexico experienced an 8.1-magnitude earthquake. Her parents died. She was shattered into a million pieces and her heart seemed to have stopped. She also thought she was dead from the earthquake's force, but then she received the happiness that her parents meant to give her. She could feel the air running through her lungs and her veins filling with red, vital blood. She was free.

A week after the tragedy, she left the hospital and decided to start her life. The country was in chaos. People were desperate for the ones lost in the dust and devastation. She didn't have anything left, only herself and her health and serenity. She needed to do something meaningful with her life, even at the young age of seventeen. But she also needed to take back the years she'd lost to all those drugs and loneliness. She decided to help the victims of the earthquake by offering her home as a mini-shelter for lost people. The people of the drug rehab center helped her with everything and she didn't have any trouble. It was amazing that she wanted to help so much, she wanted to help everyone especially people who had lost their families. She wanted people to overcome the pain and learn that it could be controlled by one's mind. She was incredibly happy, even when talking about the loss of her parents. She realized something: life is much more than loneliness. We create in ourselves loneliness when there is none. Life is full of tricks to test you, to see how far you can go, how far you can push yourself to make your dreams come true. Life is a puppet that has its tricks, and if you discover how to move it, you win. It is just a matter of control and understanding.

Stéphanie Delatour, seventeen, says that, "My passion is acting and traveling." She is enrolled in the International Baccalaureate program, and her wish is to become an actress and director of films.

SECTION SEVEN

Candlelights of Kindness and Faithfulness

Meet The Authors
L to R -Row 1: Dennis Barbato, Rodolfo Blanco.
Row 2: Katrina Ruiz, Colleen Cosgrove, Michelle Cote.
Shana Chang, Asha Hill. Row 3: Guillermo Moratorio,
Chandler Griffith, Jason Bendezu.

AN ACT OF KINDNESS
By Asha Hill

Love comes in different places and faces.
–A. Hill

I remember back when I was eleven years old—it was the summer before sixth grade, and I had just moved to Miami, Florida, from Brooklyn, New York. When I started school, things weren't going so well for me, and I prayed every night to go back to New York. When the prayers never came true, I would cry at the thought of my old home.

I do remember wanting to fit in so badly that I tried everything I could: changing my hair, clothes and even my personality, but none of this worked, and I felt worse, as a result. When I did finally make friends at school, I realized how much I meant to them. It didn't matter whether I was happy or sad, they were there for me. They cared about making me happy and even understood how much it hurt me to move, so they helped me see the best of my new home and school, and I finally felt at home.

One specific memory I have is when my best friend Amanda bought me a New York charm. She told me wherever I was to make sure that I wore it, and I would never forget my first home and how much it meant to me. She also said that as much as I love New York, I had to try and love my new home as well, so that the pain would go away. I know I will never forget what she and my other friends did for me. They told me that with them by my side, my life in Miami would be good.

This shows me that an act of kindness comes from the

heart; that it's about giving something to someone that no one can ever take away, and about making someone feel special and important. It didn't take money or luxurious things to make me that happy—just my friend's giving me the charm and telling me how she felt helped me realize I had made some great friends.

I'll always miss New York, and deep down inside I'll always wish that I was in my first home. But I can rest assured now that I have a home that is just as great. I also have friends who have taught me that love comes in different places and faces.

Asha Hill, fourteen, was born in Brooklyn, New York, where she lived for eleven years. She has written stories for several years and wanted to become a writer before focusing on her current interest in theatre. Asha is in the performing arts drama program and a member of the Caribbean Club at school, as well as a member of the hip-hop Cuda Flava dance troupe. She plans to attend college and become successful in theatre or the medical arts.

NIGHTLIGHT
By Katrina Ruiz

The black clothes sprawled on the chair,
    their pockets of despair frown at her.
Years of innocence have been stolen,
    memories linger so that she may have a chance to trace
    back a past,
but no longer can she travel in time;
    there is no alternate dimension,
only the present reality.

A single white candle flickers in her room,
    she watches shadows dance against the wall.
Her memory rewinds and she relives the instant,
    when she learns that a friend is the ultimate companion.

I watch a young soul experience the incomprehensible,
    she can do nothing but observe me.
I can feel her loving gaze and it pains me even more,
    I weep uncontrollably.
I yearn for her to help me with my hurt,
    but I do not know how to ask.
Our lives are still quite fresh,
    we are hardly a decade and a half in this world.
Yet there are times when age is not a factor,
    and thanks to my friend I learned and healed,
    with the newfound knowledge that
        compassion is the only consolation for a person.

She approaches me with a single white candle,
flickering in the darkness of my room.
She hands me the symbol and tells me,
"Take this candle and may it protect you, and comfort
you in your time of grief;
because no matter how much I wish, I know nothing
I can tell you that will make the pain disappear."

She was wrong.
at that moment I found a certain tranquility in my soul.
I looked at everything and everyone differently,
recognizing that one person's individual support
can change an entire perspective.
One small gesture.

She acknowledges the heartfelt words,
and on that one night she sleeps,
a commodity/necessity she had not indulged
in for a long period.

Katrina Ruiz wrote this poem after her grandfather's
death, so that she would "never forget that a simple gesture
such as compassion can change a person's life." She hopes
to study medicine and become a published author of poetry
and short stories.

A LOVING CHILD
By *Cristian Bossa*

*Generosity could sometimes impact a person's life and even
spare them in the bad times. -C. Bess*

On the grounds of the Small Fry Daycare Center, we came across a variety of wonderfully talented and special kids, all brought together by mommy and daddy to celebrate the art of coloring with crayons and nap time after lunch. Among these kids we found two fantastic and energetic five-year-olds named Charlie and Bobby, who were under the care of the same teacher and yet did not know each other. Charlie sat at the front of the class, almost always "reading" a book, while Bobby would be in the back on the floor, coloring with crayons on anything else he could find.

The days passed with them doing the same thing over and over, and during lunch it was the same—they sat at opposite ends of the playground. Charlie always brought his lunch in a brown paper bag, and his mommy made the same meal for him every day—his favorite, a peanut butter and jelly sandwich—along with a large red apple, orange juice and chocolate chip cookies. He never complained, because it was what he liked, even though he never ate his apple. He'd either throw it away with the bag or by itself, if he had lunch left over.

Bobby, on the other hand, was a tall five-year-old who often brought money to school to buy his lunch from the vending stands on the playground, which mostly contained junk food such as ice cream and soda, which he really liked, but he also liked fruits as well. When his mother made him lunch, it would be a cold turkey sandwich and any type of fruit. He even had more than one sandwich a day, at times, as well as more than one piece of fruit, and it didn't matter what kind—grapes, apples, oranges or strawberries—and ate every bit of it, not sharing any of it, even if other kids had none.

One morning, Bobby arrived at school with neither lunch nor lunch money. He tried to call his mommy and ask her to bring some change for him. One...two...three rings, but no one picked up at his house. His mommy was nowhere to be found. But he was a big boy, and so told no one about his situation. He was sure he could make it through the day without food, so he made it seem like everything was all right. But by lunchtime he was starving, he couldn't believe how hungry he was. His appetite increased when he saw all his friends eating, and he looked desperate and hungry.

Meanwhile, Charlie was eating his usual lunch at the other end of the playground. His lunch finished, he went to throw away his apple. As he walked, he saw Bobby's desperate look and wondered what was wrong. Not knowing any better, Charlie approached Bobby and handed him the apple, hoping it would make him feel better, but he had no idea what he had done for Bobby. Not only did he help him in a time of need, but he also changed Bobby's way of thinking. Bobby then realized how generosity could sometimes impact a person's life and even spare them in the bad times.

Bobby thought about the times he denied his friends some of his food and decided he would no longer be selfish; he would share his food. He did not thank Charlie for his good deed that day, but the next morning, Bobby approached Charlie to thank him and began what was sure to be a long-term friendship.

Cristian Bossa is a seventeen-year-old junior who is studying theatre and a member of the Florida Thespian

Society. His interests are varied, however, and he hopes to graduate from college as an accomplished engineer.

JOEY
By Michelle Cote

*For her (my mother's) caring and kindness,
I truly do love her. -M. Cote*

We were going through some hard times when it happened. My mom and I had been fighting, and I didn't want to listen to her suggestions or demands. She taunted me. I couldn't take it anymore.

One day, we got word my cousin Joey was in the hospital. I thought I had misunderstood or misinterpreted, since I had walked into a room in the middle of a conversation my mother was having and eavesdropped, although I knew I shouldn't have. I just knew I heard wrong—he was probably okay, and I was getting all worked up for nothing.

Afterwards, my mom went to her room and then my aunt called, needing to speak to her, saying that it was urgent. She was crying, and I talked to her first, trying to calm her down. I guessed she was probably with Joey at the hospital.

"Why?" I asked her, but she wouldn't tell me. My mother picked up and yelled at me to get off the phone, but I didn't want to. She came into the room I was in, still yelling at me, and I ran to my room, closing the door and picking up the phone, listening to the conversation again, and wondering what was so important that I was not allowed to hear.

I waited, and listened, then cried. Joey had cancer. "Why?" I thought. "He's only four. Why did it have to be him?" There were so many questions I wanted to ask but couldn't, and I even wondered why I was listening to my mom's private conversation. Then I heard her say we were going somewhere—to my aunt's house? No, to the hospital.

She came and told me to pack some things, since we were staying away overnight. Mother took me to my aunt's house and soon went to the hospital. I was sure my cousin Jessica knew, she just had to know, but it turned out she didn't, and maybe my aunt wouldn't tell her. But I had to know more, and so I waited up for someone to come home.

The hours passed and I fell asleep. Much later I heard a noise, and it was my mother. I asked her, "Where is he? I want to see him."

"I can't tell you," she said.

"Why?" I replied, "I am old enough to know—in fact, I already know."

She came in the room and said she'd take me to the hospital the next day. She knew I had listened, but she wasn't mad anymore, just sad and crying. She then told me everything, and we fell asleep.

Soon it was morning, the sun bright in the sky. We got up, dressed, got in the car and started the drive to the hospital. I soon saw a sign that said "Hospital—28 miles." I wondered if it could seem any farther. But soon we were there, and it came into view. I was scared now—what would Joey look like?

We parked and then went up to his room to see him, and it was nothing like I imagined. He was pale, weak and had lost most of his hair, including his eyebrows and eyelashes. He sees me and says, "Michi," then stuck out his hand and I took it. He tried to get up but he couldn't, and I cry, holding him in my arms. This stays with me and runs through my mind constantly later on.

Months passed, and Joey got better—able to get up and walk around. When we went back to the hospital to see him, he ran up to me and we played. He was happy that he could go home. And he did so. Yes, he went back home to his sisters and brothers who were happy to see him again. I watched them play together, then my mother and I went home much later on. After that, we started to work out our problems. She stopped nagging me, and I listened to her. For that, for her caring and kindness, I truly do love her.

I love Joey, and so I visit him every weekend. The two-hour drive doesn't bother us. We soon hear that he's cured—no more cancer—and we are happy. He does go for checkups every six months, but there is nothing there so far, and we think that he is cured for good.

Now, whenever we see Joey, we take him to the park, which is his favorite place to go. I swing him on the swings, and we go down the slide together. He is happy now, and so am I.

Michelle Cote, fourteen, was born and raised in Miami. She is studying drama and hopes to become an actress one day. She is also working hard to achieve her goal of attending a good college.

A LIFE-CHANGING TRIP—A LIFE-LONG FRIEND
By Jason Bendezu

*My best friend is an example of kindness found in the world
that is more precious than gold or any other ornament.*
-J. Bendezu

Everyone has been to Disney World in his or her lifetime, and if they haven't, they're missing out. I've been there so many times, and each time I find it more exciting, looking at the park in ways I hadn't before. One unforgettable time when I went there yet sticks out in my mind. It will forever represent the kindness of an individual and the caring they show, to this day.

I went to Orlando with my youth group from church one weekend for Night of Joy, a celebration for young Christians. I was not an active part of a youth group, unlike many others there, so I felt edgy, but both the leader of the group and a close friend of mine suggested I go, saying it would be a blast. I had asked if I could bring along a friend, and my friend said it was fine. So it was now set—I was going to this festival and head back to a place that had always brought me joy, not knowing how the trip would eventually turn out.

The bus ride up was spectacular. I got to sit with a bunch of my old friends from the youth group and introduce the friend I had invited to them. We all seemed to get along fine. When we got off the bus after arriving at the theme park, the smells of popcorn, clean air and unpackaged merchandise overwhelmed me, as it always does, and I smiled widely, knowing that nothing could go wrong.

It was time to separate into groups and go off on our own

into the park, and we immediately went to join with my good friend and the leader who had asked me to go. When my friend and I went to the leader (who was also a good friend) to join, he said, "Sorry, my group's full."

"What do you mean?" I asked as everyone else began moving away.

He said, "Hey, try and find another group. We'll see you inside."

I was shocked—not only because the two groups each had only ten kids, but that the leader hadn't even thought of including the one person he had invited in his group.

My friend had rejected me, and for fifteen minutes I sat with the head of the youth group ministry, trying to find a group to go with. I had even approached my brother's group, which he was leading, and was also rejected, this time by my own flesh and blood. As each group marched off into the park, my friend and I were left behind, wondering what to do. I stood there feeling even worse for my friend, because I had dragged her along and ruined her day as well, and started crying.

And then, a sort of warmth covered me, a feeling that can only be described as kindness and compassion. She wrapped her arms around me and kissed my crying eyes, saying, "I know exactly how you feel, and you know what? We can have fun on our own, just you and me. I'm happy with just you and me, if you are." I wrapped my arms around her, and we walked for a little while as I regained my composure.

She had lifted me up when I was down on both myself and my friends, and she stood strong not only for herself, but for both of us. Such an act required courage, kindness of heart and compassion for another human, and to this day, I cannot forget the way she looked at me, her smile reassuring me that all would be all right, and that the day could still be as miraculous as I expected it to be. My best friend is an example of kindness found in the world that is more precious than gold or any other ornament. In all that she takes part of in my life, I'm glad to say that I always have her by my side.

Jason Bendezu is currently a senior enrolled in the International Baccalaureate program. He enjoys watching and critiquing films, dancing and wrestling for his school team, for which he placed third in state competition this year. He feels that life's stresses can be calmed with a skip, hop and a jump back to one's childhood and the associated joys of innocence. His life motto: "Never stop learning..." He will be attending either the University of Florida or the U.S. Air Force Academy in the fall, in pursuit of a bachelor's degree in behavioral science.

A MAZE OF GRACE
By Chandler Griffith

*The naked eye cannot so easily recognize that life is,
in fact, a maze of grace.–C. Griffith*

The dictionary defines grace as a "kindly, charitable interest in others." It is unnecessary and unrequited. Perhaps that is why it is so hard to come by and seldom experienced. I discovered it at sixteen—an age when grace, charity and good deeds came together in a state of altruism that I thought I would not see until I was much older, but the less I knew about what would cause this, the more of an impact it had upon me.

The event occurred on a Sunday, a day that is normally spent at home with family or catching up on last minute tasks, but this Sunday was different in that my best friend Bobby and I were on our way home from the Miami-Dade County Youth Fair after a full day of haphazard carnival rides and fattening foods. We could think of nothing better than to get home and pass out for a few hours and en route we were surprisingly free of worry.

As we entered one of the larger intersections by my house, the light turned yellow and an oncoming car was making a left. I saw it and did the best I could to stop. I have heard the dramatic retellings of serious car accidents, and never realized the truth of all of them: everything slowed to a crawl, and I honestly did feel as though my life was going to end. My car became a mass of smoke, broken glass and two terrified teens. I could not see or hear, and all I wondered was, is Bobby all right, was it his head that had broken the windshield, and how did my arms get burned? With all these questions in my brain, the only lucid thought I had was that we needed to get out of the car.

As we got out, I was able to see the damage—the car was totaled, but we had no serious visible injuries. From out of nowhere a stranger approached us in a run, and what made me notice him was the look of concern in his eyes. He asked how we were and did all he could do to help. He said that we should move from the car and helped us regain our composure. He said, "You two look pretty shaken up—you should call your parents." We heeded his advice, never once wondered who this kind man was, this man who we knew nothing about who tried to take our minds off the incident. For a split second, I wondered what had happened to the other car, and then saw that it had flown off to the opposite side of the intersection. I figured that they would be all right and tended to the burns on my arms.

When the cops arrived, one began questioning me and the other began questioning the other man. When I tried to set things straight, saying that he had only been a bystander, I realize that not only was I wrong, but also selfish—the man had been the other driver. I asked him, "How is your car?" And he answered, "I don't know–I came to check on you." This hit me hard. He had not only forgotten everything to check on us, two strangers, and here I was feeling sorry for myself, while this man had run from his totaled car to aid a person who was in need.

This accident gave me so much insight into what makes humans tick. After such an experience, people usually come to the conclusion that life is short and can end at any time, but this was not my new philosophy. Instead, I discovered grace, which is not a run-of-the-mill-type of kindness, or one reserved only for those with a "not-for-profit" soul.

I am grateful for the accident, because it taught me and didn't hurt me. It opened my eyes to things I had never noticed, and made me see grace everywhere—in the smallest and least noticeable of human pleasures, from mother to mother, sibling to sibling and stranger to stranger. The prospects of grace are immeasurable. The point is that we may all need our own car accident in order to see the potential of a full life. The naked eye can not so easily recognize that life is, in fact, a maze of grace.

Chandler Griffith, seventeen, has not previously attempted getting published, and expresses his sympathy for anyone who has ever experienced a loss, including those most directly affected by the September 11th events.

UNEXPECTED KINDNESS
By Colleen Cosgrove

*My (self-realization) change isn't on the outside, but inside.
And I am doing it for no one else but myself.* -C. *Cosgrove*

Throughout our lives, we have all had major occurrences that have severely altered our lives, and though it seemed, at the time, to have swayed us from our goal, we have proceeded. Not too long ago, this was the case for me—no progression or significant life alteration, but a whole new perspective brought about by one person. As I look back, that one person should have been myself, but it wasn't. It was my teacher, much to my surprise.

I'll start at the beginning. I am an out-of-place-type of kid; I don't want to fit in at all, nor have I wanted or tried to, and still don't. I used to think of myself as mediocre and just plain "blah," so I never tried or cared, destined for a mediocre life, in my eyes.

One day in my chemistry class, my teacher handed us back our grades for an assignment and I had a 40. I was okay with that, though, and just shrugged it off as the best I could do (our grades were listed by I.D. numbers and not names), until some kid says, "Oh, my God, who is the idiot with a 40? I feel sorry for them." And I remember thinking, "Don't feel sorry for me—I feel sorry for you wasting all your time studying."

With that thought, I walked out of the class to deliver a CD to a teacher whom I often disagreed with in class; so I wasn't looking forward to this particular visit. I arrived at his door, already ticked off. I waited until he opened it, with a goofy grin on his face, then saw the serious look on my face. I don't know exactly what it was in his look that got me, but I just started bawling, with tears streaming down my face, and I left before I said something I would regret.

Later in the day, I calmed down a bit after eating lunch and trying to forget my failure, when it was time for that particular teacher's class. I wondered what I was supposed to say to him, how was I supposed to justify my tears? You just didn't cry without a reason—it's not allowed. So I walked in and took a seat—quiet, solemn and kind of nervous. Though I had calmed down, I found myself on the edge of tears again, and he hadn't even looked at me. His desk area was swarming with students as usual, since he was a popular and well-liked teacher, perhaps too busy with other people's problems to deal with mine. He had probably forgotten about me already.

When the bell rings, everyone takes seats. Then the teacher announces silent reading time, looks at me and motions me out to the hallway. I was going to tell him that it was no big deal, end of story, and I promised myself I wouldn't cry. But what happened was the exact opposite of my wishes, as I broke down and told him everything, finding I could relate to him, and I needed to do that. But I didn't care, right? Wrong. I found that my problem was that I cared too much, but I didn't have either the discipline or persistence to address it properly—I needed an audience.

As if I had said it out loud, he offered it to me, which was a pure miracle. Even still, I had my doubts, thinking, "He has so many other students to help, with so many other things to do—dinner to make for his wife, hockey to play with his team. This could never work." I figured that he'd be patient and dedicated for a week, then his interest would fade. I had been through it before, so I wasn't all that excited and was sure that as soon as he saw the tears were gone, he would move on.

I was wrong. He was not only determined to see me learn the knowledge, he also wanted to see the results, and he had given me a reason why: Incentive for my future. I couldn't believe that for so long I thought that I was just going to slip into the crowd for the year. I knew now I was special, and I was going to show the world. No one knows it yet, and probably never will, since my change isn't on the outside, but inside. And I am doing it for no one else but myself.

Colleen Cosgrove, seventeen, is currently working at Parrot Jungle. On the weekends she loves going to concerts with her best friend Jeni. She says she "hopes to attend a West Coast college next year and surf every day."

MOTHER: ANOTHER WORD FOR KINDNESS
By Dennis Barbato

<u>Mother:</u> *a woman as related to her child or children; a female parent.*

To a teenager, the word "mother" may not sound very comforting and special, but in my case it does. My mom and I have always had a close relationship, but recently something changed in our relationship and made it even better. Growing up, she was always there for me to talk to, confide in and make me smile. Usually throughout their teen years, people tend to fight with their parents, but my mom makes it impossible for that to happen, and that was all due to our relationship—I could always tell her what was on my mind.

Over the summer before my senior year, many things changed in my life. It was then that I came out to her. There had been so many times in the past where the subject of being gay would come up, and I would avoid it and not tell her, and I wasn't sure why, even with her being easy to talk to and the knowledge that she would love me, no matter what—I just wasn't comfortable telling her that her only son was gay. But one day that all changed. It was difficult and awkward to confirm this to her, even though it may have always been in the back of her mind.

The day was August 23, 2001, and she and I had gone to pick up my senior pictures together. On the ride home, we were just talking about life in general and everything about it. I started talking about trusting people with things, and she told me that I could trust her with anything. I had come so close before, always shaking and unable to do so, but that day felt right, so after we got home and started looking at the pictures, I just told her. I broke into tears after telling her because I wasn't sure how she'd react. All I remember was her crying as well and coming over to give me a hug, one that gave me the best and most special feeling ever. She thought I was crying because I wasn't happy with myself, but that was not the case. I just wondered why I had waited so long to tell her.

We talked about it, and she asked me different questions about matters she wasn't sure about dealing with being gay, which was an amazing talk. She soon figured out that a certain someone she thought was just a close friend was actually someone special. She had figured him for my boyfriend, and even wanted to call him and tell him that she accepted and supported us both. That really made me feel at peace, and she then called my dad and sister to tell them, and they have been so supportive.

My mom still reminds me how proud she is of me and says, "You're still my baby." I recall thinking that it would be so weird to talk to her about it, especially about guys, but it hasn't been, and she has surprised me with how well she has taken everything. The main reason I had not told her before was because I wasn't comfortable with myself, and only after I gained it was it time to tell her. My life has been so much easier since then, with my family and especially my mom.

No one should ever doubt or belittle themselves, and since coming out to her all my life has changed, and knowing that she is happy with me makes me happy. Without her, I wouldn't even be here, nor would I be the person I am. It feels good for me to say that she is proud of me, and that I love her more than words can express. I owe her more than I can ever give in a lifetime of living, and I am happy to call her "Mom."

Dennis Barbato, a senior, is anxious to graduate and begin his life as a student at Florida International University. He hopes one day to become successful in the advertising industry. He is grateful for the incredible people who have blessed his life thus far. He sends love to his mother, his family and his friends.

WHAT CHANGED MY LIFE
By Rodolfo Blanco

"Kindness is love in action. It unites families."

Something that changed my life occurred when I went to Canada. I went there with my family; so did my aunt and my two cousins, as well as her friend. It changed our lives because we became closer on this trip than we were before, even though we went everywhere together. Every night the parents would play cards or chess and games like that, while the kids were in the room playing different things.

When we went skiing I took care of one of my cousins, who was ten years old. In doing this, we stayed together while skiing for the whole time. The first time we were up there at the mountain, my cousin and I got stuck because we did not know how to ski, so we followed two little kids down the hill. But those kids were good enough to go down the expert mountain: we did not know that when we followed them. So, we ended up falling all the way down the mountain.

After that, we went and got some snacks and picked up a map, so we could find where the easy slopes were. We still fell a lot and kept on falling for a while, but we got better and the second time we tried, we barely fell. I grew a lot closer to him from this experience. Afterward, we went back to the hotel and ate in the private lobby with the rest of our group, like the big family we are.

The trip we took to Canada brought me and my family closer, which is the main reason I loved it. Now we call and talk to each other much more often than before.

Rodolfo "Rudy" Blanco, fifteen, is a Florida Thespian. He intends to attend college and major in theatre arts.

CHANGING AN ATTITUDE
By Shana Chang

*I have learned to look beneath the surface,
and the experience (of feeling grateful) changed
the way I look at life.* -S. Chang

December of 2000 would be a month I could never forget. I had a chance to take a look into a world that I didn't know about. On a field trip, my youth group and I went to an orphanage to donate food and presents. During my visit, I was able to talk and interact with some of the children.

As I got to know them, little by little, I realized how fortunate I was. My life was good, I had a roof over my head, my parents loved me, and I had nothing to complain about.

Later that day, we watched as the kids opened the presents we had brought. It was great to see the happiness on their faces. We left that day contented with our intentions and good deeds.

Never again will I take for granted the little things in life. I have learned to look beneath the surface, and the experience changed the way I look at life.

Shana Chang is enrolled in the drama magnet program. She enjoys performing the various plays and helping to produce the technical aspects of the shows. At fifteen, she is keeping her options open and considering acting, directing or reporting as possible careers.

HOW TO FEEL NEAT
By Guillermo Moratorio

*Kindness can take you out of the cold and surround your
body with heat. -G. Moratorio*

You see them as you're walking,
As you're moving down the street.
It's those random acts of kindness
From people you've yet to meet.

It could be seeing a fallen friend
And helping him off the concrete.
Or someone asking for a piece of paper
And you give her your last sheet.

It's these random acts of kindness
That make us all complete.
It makes you feel all good inside
From your head down to your feet.

When you give someone else your lunch
And are left with nothing to eat
You are full with a sense of pride and joy
And that is the best treat.

And if you don't get what I'm saying
Then your mind is off a beat
Kindness can take you out of the cold
And surround your body with heat.

So the next time you see someone down
Whether it be in hail, snow or sleet
Say, "Hello there, how are you?"
And the both of you will feel pretty neat.

*Guillermo Moratorio, seventeen, is a junior and president
of his thespian troupe. While he greatly enjoys acting on stage,
he thinks he would like to have a career as a United Parcel
Service (UPS) driver.*

SECTION EIGHT

$\mathscr{C}$andlelights of Kindness and Gentleness

Meet The Authors
L to R-Row 1: Francisco Trigueros, Erica Naess, Marianne
Cerda, Morayo Faleyimu. Row 2: Monica Palenzuela,
Stephanie Martinez. Row 3: Jeanette Ramos, Daniel
Krugliak, Veronica Gonzalez.

HE SANG A SWEET SONG
By Stephanie Martinez

"Kindness anticipates others' needs and wishes."

All sounds seemed muffled and distant from inside the stuffy practice room where she stood trembling. This young American girl, lacking confidence and self-esteem, had just advanced to the semifinals in a prestigious international music competition. She walked the halls, listening to the sizable voices of her competition and, feeling immensely intimidated, she retreated to the stifling room.

The girl had been singing all her life. She loved to sing— yet she felt unworthy and undeserving of such a distinguished event. Back home she received praise for her talent, but this wasn't Miami, Florida. This was Japan. The musicians whom she would be competing against came from all ends of the globe, from Australia to England to America, and everywhere in between.

"What am I doing here?" she contemplated. She exercised feelings of guilt as she recalled the numerous sponsorships and donations from her community that assisted in funding her trip. So many people. She felt the pressure bearing down on her chest and shoulders, squeezing the air out of her lungs. Such distress was enough to make one cringe at the sight of her, beauty distorted by the pressure of nerves.

A few minutes in the congested practice room was enough to send the wreck of a girl outside, gasping for air. As she took in a breath, she heard a magnificent sound coming from the room next door; a beautiful tenor voice, thick and rich in tone. The sound mesmerized her, drawing her closer and closer to the door. The voice blasted a glorious note in the upper range, and the girl was drawn even closer to the door of the room. Tentatively, she peered in. The music stopped. Without warning, the door swung violently open and the girl stood alarmed and abashed at being discovered. Surprisingly enough, out strolled the young man with the marvelous, mature voice.

"I was just listening to you sing. You have a beautiful voice," the girl commented with an embarrassed smile, as she cautiously proceeded to escape the situation. Spying on the competition was like a crime against your own kind. It is an unspoken rule—something you don't do. Yet, the innocent young American unintentionally found herself in a most unfortunate set of circumstances, and she desperately wanted to flee. She had been taking small steps backward, her breathing was heavy and her face spelled despondency. She turned to make her getaway, but before she knew it, the young man had gotten hold of her arm. She looked on with terror, thinking of the possible consequences.

The young man had a commanding presence as he stared at the girl with confusion in his eyes. Silence enveloped the hall. After an awkward moment, the young man finally cut in and in broken English said, "Hello. My name is Long Cai Hunt. Hunt, like Hunter. I'm from Malaysia."

"Hello," answered the girl.

"I heard you," he said. "Pretty voice."

The girl let out a soft uncomfortable laugh, relieving some tension. She thanked Cai for the compliment and told him her name.

"I'm Stephanie from America," she said, and the two began a dialogue.

At an international competition in the performing arts, where vigorous competitive nature so often dominates, Cai had done the virtually unthinkable. With a disposition most friendly, he embraced a fellow competitor, complemented, conversed, and even sang with her. Stephanie's lack of self-regard and self-assurance would have presented no threat to Long Cai Hunt in competition had he not taken her under his wing. Yet, his gentle nature and kind spirit would not allow him to isolate his frightened, fragile peer.

For the next six days of competition, Cai took Stephanie in, acting as a friend, motivator and cheerleader all at once.

The two formed an inseparable bond. He would watch her practice and continuously encourage her and remark on the great amount of talent and potential she possessed. In his charming broken English he taught her how to use chopsticks and speak words in Malay, Chinese and Mandarin. He acted as her translator, assisting her in socializing with other musicians. He never allowed her to be cold, always offering up his jacket, even though the chilly weather could very well affect his voice. Cai was unusually well mannered for a boy his age and had refreshing charisma. He was tender with Stephanie; yet, interestingly enough, their relationship was not romantic. It was that of a true friendship, one in which both parties look out for each other without jealousy or malice, but with genuine kindness.

On the first day of competing, both Cai and Stephanie were slightly nervous. Yet, in accordance with his usual benevolence, Cai was generous enough to negotiate and find Stephanie a private practice room where she could rehearse comfortably. She performed splendidly, as did he. That night, as the university announced the names of those musicians who would move on to the next level, it was incredibly touching to see that out of 94 vocalist entrants, Stephanie Benitez and Long Cai Hunt were two of the seven names called as finalists.

The next day, before her performance at the finals, and with much apprehension, Stephanie began yielding to her original lack of confidence and self-esteem, almost losing the strength that Cai helped instill in her. Yet, as soon as he noticed her begin to panic, he stopped his own practice, went to her side, massaged the tension out of her shoulders, and calmly mumbled some inspiring words, telling her to relax.

That night, Stephanie gave her most brilliant performance ever. She was able to release all the pressure, all the fear, and all the feelings of inadequacy and sing from the heart. She overcame many significant obstacles that night to sing like never before and received a vast amount of acclamation. She was awarded a special prize at the competition for "abundant creative ability and artistic endeavors" along with a monetary prize. She and Cai shared a poignant embrace in celebration, as she was recognized by many notable musicians and requested for several significant performances. However, in the whirlwind of acclaim, Stephanie did not lose sight of the young man to whom she owed a credible amount of her success.

In six memorable days, Cai was able to transform a shy, insecure young girl into a strong, confident young woman. All it took was an act of kindness and an act of faith. Cai did not have to sacrifice his time and energy to help a vulnerable girl, whom he met while she spied on his rehearsal. He did not have to befriend a competitor and threaten his chances of winning an international competition by encouraging and motivating her. He did not have to sacrifice his health and vocal ability for her well-being. He did not have to do anything, but he did it anyway, and he did it with kindness, he did it with compassion, and he did it with love. Cai believed in Stephanie when she didn't believe in herself, and because of his simple act of kindness...she is forever changed.

Stephanie Martinez aspires to be an opera singer, but clings to her passion for writing. She has performed in the Florida Youth Chorale at Carnegie Hall, toured Europe as a featured vocal soloist, and was awarded the Hironake Heisuke Award at the 7th Takasaki International Art & Music Competition in Japan.

AN ANGEL DANCES
By Daniel Krugliak

David's strength and love for life is what kept him alive.
-D. Krugliak

Ever since I could remember I have been going to Synagogue to hear the songs of the Torah. I am Jewish, but this story is not about me. It's about a man, a great man. Every Jewish holiday, either Chanukah or Passover, that man would be there in Synagogue singing his heart out so even the angels could not miss hearing him. Every holiday in Synagogue the whole congregation would get up and dance around him and sing with him.

It was not until the day he was on his deathbed that I heard the story from my mom of why we danced around this man. It began during World War II when the Nazi Germans were taking over Poland. They had already sent hundreds of Jews to their death by this time. The Nazis entered several villages, destroying everything in sight. One village in Poland in particular was different from all the rest because of a little six-year-old boy named David. He and his mother had gone to Synagogue on Friday to pray, just as they did any other Friday. But this was not like any other Friday.

As David and his mother stood up to pray and dance to the melody of the Torah, the Nazi soldiers barged into their sanctuary pulling out their guns. The Nazis then shot into the air, yelling for everyone to come out and line up. Women and children on one side and men on the other. Tears started to fly following bullets. As David stood in line crying he pulled on his mother's dress to ask how come they were not dancing. His mother did not answer. He again pulled his mother's dress to ask his question, which was almost lost in all the mayhem. Again she did not answer as tears fell from her face.

As the boy asked again, almost in a pleading way, a Nazi soldier came walking by. He laughed at him and said, "Stupid Jew, you want to dance? Go dance," and pulled his arm and threw him and four other children on the ground. Then he said to them to get up and dance and told everyone to watch. So the five children, including little David, danced. They danced their hearts out. As the giggling and laughter grew from the children, that same Nazi soldier pulled his trigger back and shot the girl dancing with David.

The Nazi yelled to keep dancing so they did and, again, another child was shot. They kept on dancing with their hands raised to the heavens and their spirits high. They danced and danced. Then another was shot and another. Poor little David was left alone standing in the middle of his dead friends, but to everyone's surprise, even to the Nazis, he kept dancing. His arms were raised to the heavens as he danced. Everyone, including his mother, started to clap a rhythm. It was hypnotic, everyone's fear and sorrow was lifted by the little boy's love and zest for life. The Nazi soldier shouted and demanded everyone stop. The soldier then grabbed the boy and said, "You stupid boy, who do you think you are dancing with?"

David replied, "With the angels."

David was one of the millions who were in the Holocaust. David's strength and love for life is what kept him alive. David was eleven when the Jews were liberated. He grew up and married and made a life for himself. Everyone knew his story. They knew who David was. So I learned that day why everyone danced around him. He was our angel.

Daniel Krugliak, says, "I felt it was important to get this story out," and believes it shows "what a Candlelight story should be like." One of a set of triplets, Daniel. seventeen, also says, "Drama is my passion in life. I hope this story will touch people like it has touched me."

THE REALITY OF THEATRE
By Lauren Daniels

Through the theatre I discovered that I could access different sides of myself. -L. Daniels

It is hard to believe that my theatre career is almost over. I owe so much of who I am to the theatre. As a shy twelve-year-old, I sat in my first auditorium at Southwood Middle School, devoid of all company, waiting there, for my audition to begin. I had never done a monologue before; I had never auditioned before. I had never done anything like this before! Every one before me seemed so professional, so rehearsed.

I had never wanted to audition. I was terminally high-strung; crying if my mom was even five minutes late to pick me up. She thought that acting would force me to go with the flow, and I didn't disagree. After the monologue was finished, I walked back to my seat, feeling vulnerable and exposed. The torture was not over. Once the monologues had concluded it was time for improvisations.

I did not know what an improvisation was, but I quickly learned. By far, this was worse than the monologue. At least with that I had time to prepare–now it was spur of the moment. I am a Capricorn, a planner; it was as if they took me out of the kiddy pool and threw me into the depths of the ocean. It was my turn. We received our situation...a hair salon. They chose me to be the stylist and the other two girls to be customers. I don't remember the improv itself but I do remember the feeling–complete freedom. It was as if I had lost all sense of myself and became that hairdresser. It was at that moment I knew I wanted to do this, whether it was for two years or two minutes.

I waited anxiously for the acceptance letter and it seemed like eons went by before it arrived. On the day it arrived, I decided that it didn't matter what that piece of paper said, I would find a way to continue acting–with our without this magnet school. Fortunately, I was accepted to the drama program. There I would receive intensive theatre training along with a strong, core curriculum.

Slowly I relaxed into the "artist's" lifestyle. My mother could be late without me going into a complete panic attack. Through the theatre I discovered that I could access different sides of myself. That one moment opened up a world of possibilities for me, but I now feel that I have exhausted them. I am prepared to open a new chapter, face new challenges. I plan to take all that I have learned in theatre and apply it in other arenas. For that reason, theatre will always be a large part of my life because it is a large part of me.

Lauren Daniels has been an active member of the International Thespian Society for three years, earning the position of senior class representative. She will attend Florida State University in the fall of 2002, majoring in public relations and journalism.

UNITE
By Veronica Gonzalez

She touched everybody's life in one way or another.
–V. Gonzalez

When someone dies, everyone is sad, of course, but one person's death and her struggle for her life left her family and friends happy in one way or another. My Aunt Sharon died of cancer a few years ago when I was ten, but her constant happiness and enjoyable attitude still lingers throughout the family. When she was a child it was discovered that she had cancer behind one of her eyes. Because of this, she had to have it removed and a glass eye took its place. This never bothered her. She was extremely carefree. She never hated anyone and always saw a positive resolution to every problem. Sharon went on living her life happily. The cancer hadn't bothered her in years. She became a marine biologist and was happily married to my Uncle George. Later they had a son named Christopher, who is one year older than I am. Three or four years after he was born, Sharon and George were divorced. The constant visits of Sharon's mother agitated George to the ultimate. He had disliked Sharon's mother from the moment he met her.

Soon after all this happened, Sharon found out she had breast cancer. She went through all of the cancer treatments, one result of which is always loss of hair. Nevertheless, she stayed strong and accepted the baldness. Most people would wear a wig or a hat, but Sharon never did. She didn't care what other people thought of her. She was her own person. After this happened and her cancer had gotten worse, she had to undergo more treatment for the next couple of years.

At this time, her son was being extremely cruel to everyone. He had a gigantic attitude problem and hardly had any friends. He was very close to his mother and it was hard for him to see her go through all this pain. Every year for Christmas we would all go to my grandmother's house; every year Sharon was worse and worse. Christopher was too.

One summer everything went to extremes. Their house became uninhabitable, thought they continued to live in it. Their car was unusable as well. My cousin Chris spent the night at my house a lot. Sharon just kept getting worse. Her sister Patty even came down from Alabama to be with her, but she couldn't handle the deterioration of the house. They put it up for sale and went to live with Sharon's other sister Linda, who had plenty of space for Sharon, Chris and Patty. The couple of weeks that Sharon lived in Linda's house had been the most agonizing days for Sharon, and for everyone else who loved her, too. She had gotten to the point where she needed a nurse and had a hospital bed and other equipment brought in for her. She was on her deathbed. One day she was talking to Linda about her funeral. She didn't want a funeral, she said, she wanted a party–an Irish one (she was Irish), with plenty of beer for everyone.

My cousin was still behaving as horribly as he could, maybe even worse. But one night while he was at my house, he was taking a shower and I passed by the bathroom door and I heard him crying. He was crying with so much emotion, it was hard for me to listen to him. It made me cry myself. The next day my mom and her friend who had missed Sharon's birthday went to see her. Sharon was partially awake. My mom told her that her friend wanted to say happy belated birthday to her and Sharon smiled lightly. They started to sing "Happy Birthday" to her very softly and in the middle of the song, Sharon passed away.

Everyone was devastated. But they knew that wherever

she was now, she would be at peace. Her battle with cancer had finally ended. Her funeral "party" was just the way she wanted it. At one point they passed a microphone around for people to say good thoughts and memories about Sharon. It was a tear-jerker, but it brought everyone together. She touched everybody's life in one way or another. Now every Christmas, we still think about "Teetee Sharon" (that's what we always called her) and we miss her.

Veronica Gonzalez is a sophomore. She is interested in all the costume and make-up aspects of theatre. In the future, she intends to pursue a design career.

I'M SORRY
By Jeanette Ramos

*No kiss is worth losing the love of your life over,
or for that matter, nothing is worth that. -J. Ramos*

My stomach dropped when I came upon one of his old letters. It had fallen out while I was looking in my junk drawer rummaging through papers, birthday cards and old letters. I was looking for my birthday money that I had left in one of my cards. I would never have guessed that I would turn up one of his old letters. I read it with much love and compassion because I know that he is one person I will never forget.

It was the first day of school and I was with my best friend. We were just walking around, chatting and checking out the surroundings. You know, the normal thing to do on the first day of school. The bell rang and we reported to our first-period room. There stood a gorgeous guy. He caught my attention right away and, as luck would have it, my best friend knew him and immediately introduced us. This probably sounds naive, but I knew right then that I was going to end up liking him.

It turned out he was in two of my classes and he sat right next to me in both of them. It was all set. We became really close friends after a while and I found out that not only did I think he was good looking, but I loved his personality. As fate would have it, we eventually became a couple and our relationship was great. We spent as much time together as possible and we never got bored with each other.

We graduated from middle school together, but things were about to change. You see, I had been accepted into a magnet high school and he was going to a different high school. We decided to stay together and he told me, "Look at this as a test. A test of how strong our love is for each other." I never thought that you could fall in love at a young age, but here I was, fifteen years old and in love.

Two months into high school we broke up. He said he needed to figure things out. Sure enough, he did and pretty soon he wanted me back. We continued going out for another year after that and then I made a mistake that I will regret for the rest of my life. I had met a boy who, ironically enough, went to the same school as my boyfriend. At the end of one night, we found ourselves kissing, but I immediately regretted it. I told him that nothing could ever happen between us because I had a boyfriend whom I loved. Nevertheless, what had happened got back to my boyfriend and we broke up.

I will never know how our relationship would have developed if I hadn't done what I did. It taught me a valuable lesson. No kiss is worth losing the love of your life over, or for that matter, nothing is worth that. Maybe one day we will get back together, but for now I am moving on with my life and making sure that I don't make the same mistake twice. He will never know how much he meant to me and how much I learned from him. To him I say the only thing I can say, "I'm sorry."

Jeanette Ramos says she is "extremely interested in all aspects of theatre." A sophomore, she plans to become an actress on stage and in films. She is excited about having her story published in the Candlelights collection!

THE HANDS OF TIME
By Marianne Cerdá

*Time...I hate its inevitability. TICK TICK TICK, in my ear,
as if it's trying to warn me of something.*

September 11, 2001, at 8:45 AM, my World History class is discussing the far-fetched possibility of a World War III. September 11, 2001, at 9:25 AM, I decide to use the restroom. September 11, 2001, at 9:30 AM, upon my return from the restroom I walk into a classroom of 42 frightened faces. World War III...far-fetched? September eleventh of the year two thousand and one shall never be forgotten.

On this day terrorists attacked America. Four commercial planes were hijacked, two slamming into the World Trade Center, one hitting the Pentagon, and the last crashing outside of Pittsburgh. Less than an hour later, both towers collapsed. I watched it happen on the television; from afar it looked just like a movie...but the truth was far from a movie. It was New York City. I was left speechless. As the cameras got closer and closer to the buildings before they collapsed, they revealed the great numbers of people hanging from their windows, waving anything they could get hold of to let us know that they were still alive...and scared beyond words. A number of them took their lives by jumping from their windows a hundred floors up. It was either that or burning to death. We watched the "cookie crumble," claiming the lives of thousands. Why were we so helpless?

Now New York is covered with ash, covered with the remains of what was once a center of success, progress and life. I am so sad...what words describe the feelings of those who lost a loved one, a part of themselves? We are now left in a state of confusion. What comes next? The world is going to change. As vague and mind-blowing as it may seem, it is true. Is ignorance bliss when reality is unfolding? I'm afraid to open my eyes to the truth, but I have to...we have to...together.

Time...I hate its inevitability...but I know it's coming...so I will accept it.

Marianne Cerdá is a senior in the International Baccalaureate program. She will graduate in the top 6% of her class and will attend the University of Florida this fall. Marianne has been dancing since the age of three, and she hopes to pursue a career as a professional dancer. She would like to thank her drama teacher, Mrs. Mederos, "for everything she has done" for her.

WAITING FOR BUMBLEBEES
By Morayo Faleyimu

My cousin told me this story about her co-worker,
while she was driving me to school.

My father is coming home soon," she said again. "He just can't find a taxi."

The girl's mother was in tears. "She won't stop saying that! I've tried, and I've tried, but she just won't stop asking me when he is coming home."

Dr. Brandeis leaned toward the small girl. "Well, Angela and I will just talk. Right, Angela? We will set things straight, Ms. Lochet-Anderson."

The mother cried into a handkerchief and walked out of the office. Shelves of books covered the office walls: all warehouses of logic and reason. There were two chairs. Dr. Brandeis faced his prized Voltaire portrait, with "Reason above all" written near the bottom. Angela leaned back in her chair, staring out the window to the glassy ocean of Rockburrow, Maine. She and her mother had moved to the town after the September 11th bombing. Before that, the Anderson family had lived in a spacious New York City apartment. Every day-before that day-Angela's father had taken a bus to work, and the taxi back home. On that day, he had gone in early to work, at the World Trade Center, to finish some paperwork before hurrying home to take the family out to dinner. A month later, there was still no trace of him, but that did not keep Angela from her persistent vigil on the doorstep of her apartment building.

"My father is coming home soon. He just can't find a

taxi," she would explain to the passerby. They would smile at the image of the five-year-old girl standing ever so patiently, scanning each passing car and truck for that special figure.

Her mother did not hold the same hope.

After a few weeks, her mother got a special lock for the door, too high for Angela to reach, so she could not go out to the doorstep. But this lock could not block the memories that surfaced in the mother's sleep. Eventually, tired of the insomnia and the gnawing pain of loneliness, she packed their life into ten large boxes and drove them to Maine. On the way, Angela would track the cars, looking for taxis (her father called them bumblebees). She tried to get her mother to join the search.

"Mama, do you see any bumblebees?"

"Angie. Please."

As the drive continued, the girl became quieter and quieter. When they finally arrived, they stayed at Angela's grandparents' home, where Angela tiptoed around the dusty furniture and spoke to no one. Angela's grandfather suggested Dr. Brandeis-a family friend and psychologist-as the solution to her muteness.

"Angela? What would you like to talk about today?" Dr. Brandeis asked.

She blew a few dust motes until they spun like whirlwinds. "Nothing."

That was how the Monday, Wednesday and Friday sessions usually began and continued for an entire hour. This week was the fourth, and Dr. Brandeis was ready to admit defeat.

"Angela? What would you like to talk about today?"

Recently, she had begun the habit of asking impossible questions for the doctor to answer. This day was no exception.

"Do phones work in heaven?" she asked, adjusting the huge shirt she was wearing. (It had been her father's.)

"Well, I don't know about that. Where did you hear about

that idea?"

She shrugged. "I was just thinking." Angela chewed her lips for a few moments. "I don't have anything else to say. Can I go home now?"

Dr. Brandeis sighed, "You're free to go; let me call your mother to come pick you up."

He went home that night to his empty house, worrying over the poor child with the large eyes and wild imagination. Rummaging around in the refrigerator, he found a can of noodle soup amid a mob of takeout boxes. Outside, the water was crashing on the shore, sucking the sand dollars and shells back into the water. He walked outside with his cup of noodle soup in tow. The deck chairs were dry, so he chose the one nearest the water. He watched one wave roll a peach-and-cream conch shell up and down the beach. The shell tumbled back and forth, finally coming to rest against a large rock. It seemed to be a thing of perfection. Dr. Brandeis walked down the deck stairs, onto the sand, and picked up the shell. Mauve ridges rose and fell along the shell's side and top. The sound of the ocean's roar echoed in his head as he placed the shell in his ear and thought of Angela's words. Are there phones in heaven?

The next morning, he drove to the Lochet home. His sole passenger in the car was the conch shell wrapped in tissue paper inside a yellow box fastened with the auto-regulation seatbelt. Angela was building a sand castle down at the water's edge. She seemed oblivious to the world, in her too-big plaid shirt and dirt-smudged cheeks. Dr. Brandeis squatted beside her.

"Hello, Angela. I just came back to see how you were doing."

"Hmmpph," she answered, poking a castle tower with her stick.

"I was thinking about the question you asked me last time. About telephones in heaven."

She looked up with interest.

"I think there are telephones in heaven, but they can't call down to regular phones."

"What kind of phone do I need?" she asked. "I only have three dollars."

The doctor smiled and handed over the yellow box. "I got one for you. It's free."

Angela eagerly took the box and ripped it open.

"It's a shell."

"Put it to your ear."

She did and heard the roar of the ocean. And beneath that, she heard the sound of a familiar voice, filled with the same gravelly affection that she missed so dearly. Dr. Brandeis walked away to allow her privacy. He was surprised the shell idea had worked; he figured that she would reject the gift, but she seemed to be taking it quite seriously. Angela, he was certain, was hearing only what she wanted to hear in the shell. The girl walked in and out of the ocean waves, still talking into the shell. Finally after a few more minutes, she walked back to the doctor and handed him the shell.

"Thank you," she wiped the tears from her eyes. Some of it had already trickled down to her dirt-smudged cheeks. "I talked to my daddy. He said he can't come home now, but he can watch over me because he's an angel now."

Dr. Brandeis cradled the shell in his hand. "Take it, Angela, it's for you."

"That's okay, you can keep it now," she said, spun on her heel, and ran into the house.

The doctor regarded the shell with interest. Could she really have—? No, that was impossible. Still, he found himself lifting the shell toward his ear, wondering if he would catch the end of some ghostly communication. He heard the roar of the ocean and below that, the quiet voice of a man talking.

"Reason above all," he muttered, and wondered if that

statement could be amended.

Morayo Faleyimu is a senior who is planning to be either a writer or an editor in the future. Her favorite author is J. D. Salinger. She says he inspired her "to write stories that rely on dialogue and little narration to convey meaning." She is currently compiling a book of short stories.

STEPS
By Monica Palenzuela

The grand adventure begins
The troubles, joys, and loves that lie ahead are unknown
Thank you for your time, love, compassion and drive
For without you my life would have been empty, incomplete
My heart would not have felt what it was like
to experience love and joy
The trials we've experienced have allowed us to grow,
to bloom
Never having to look back in misery or regret,
but in fondness and longing
Never having to change anything and living each day
to its fullest
We begin to take these steps, little by little
Beginning to crawl before we walk, to walk before we run
The journey that lies ahead, unknown and challenging
A continuous mystery, a new adventure awaiting us
Our entire hearts and souls will go into this journey
We will never look back in sorrow, never in disappointment
Always with heads lifted high and a new light of hope
beaming in our hearts
Remembering the times we've spent together and
cherishing them all.

Monica Palenzuela, seventeen, is a senior and has lived in Miami for fifteen years. She is very involved in the drama program at her school and wishes to continue her study of theatre when she begins undergraduate studies at New York University in the fall of 2002.

A LIFE-LEARNED LESSON
By Francisco Trigueros

Friends are not always there for you, not like family.
-F. Trigueros

Throughout most of her 16 years, Serena McKinnels had always had what she called, "a great group of friends." She also was popular in high school, a good student and she had a family she loved very much. Serena's life was pretty much perfect, or at least that's what she thought.

However, one thing Serena didn't have in her life was a love interest. She had been secretly eyeing James Daniels, star quarterback of her high school football team and word was, James was interested in Serena as well. Eventually, Serena and James started dating, and throughout school they were known as the perfect couple, perfect for each other, or so they thought.

One day, Serena told her friends James had been pressuring her for sex and that he was becoming very persistent. Serena's friends advised her to have sex with him. Even though Serena wasn't sure that was what she wanted to do, she followed her friends' advice and finally slept with James.

Around three weeks later Serena invited her best friends over, saying she urgently had to talk with them. Once Anne, Christina, Janie and Jessica were there, she told them the news. She was pregnant. A heartbroken Serena told her friends she didn't know what to do, that James had broken up with her and was not going to help her in any way. But the response Serena got from her friends was one she did not expect.

Her "best friends," who had vowed to "always be there" for her were now telling her it was all her fault and that she should've known better than to sleep with him, when she didn't want to do it. Of course, Serena knew that she was responsible, in part, but her friends were the ones who had so insistently pushed her to do it, just like James did. Then those good friends left her alone saying, "It's your life, not ours; we don't want anything to do with you." And so Serena was left all alone, heartbroken, betrayed and pregnant.

But out of all this drama had come a good thing, a life lesson. Serena now knew that friends are not always there for you, not like family. When Serena told her family the news, unlike James or her girl friends, they did not leave her. They were there for her, every step of the way.

As for James, he graduated with one of the lowest GPA's of his class. When word got around that year that he only wanted girls so he could sleep with them, very few girls would speak to him at all; and because of his low grades, he was pulled out of the football program.

Serena, on the other hand, decided to have her baby. With the help of her family she went on to UCLA and got masters degrees in business and engineering. Even though she had gone through a very hard time in her life, she realized that with the help of her family, who really loved her, she now had a daughter she loved very much and a promising career ahead of her. She had also met some new friends along the way. Now she knew that, no matter what they said, she was always going to take responsibility for herself. And now her main focus was her daughter for whom she thanked God every day.

Francisco Trigueros is interested in pursuing an acting career in the future. For the moment, this sophomore student enjoys learning about the technical side of theatrical productions.

PLEASE DON'T CRY
By *Monique Parris*

*Your lovingkindness has helped me grow in the ways that I
have needed. —M. Parris*

You were always there, no matter what was going on in
your life. You always protected me from so many wrongs.
And now, as part of my growing up, I have to leave this, oh,
so familiar place.

Please don't cry. I'm taking every lesson you taught me
with me to the next level. No matter what I do or where I go,
your lessons will be with me. Your words of encouragement
will echo in the wind. Even now I feel your presence always
in the rain.

Please don't cry. Don't worry, I'll take care of myself.
Please don't cry. Your time to take care of me is over. Please
don't cry. I know that it's sad. But you always knew that this
time was coming, so know that it's here; why be sad and blue?
We knew this day would dawn.

Please don't cry, or I'll cry too, and it's really not all that
sad. But if you must, then cry because I'm all grown up!
Your lovingkindness has helped me grow in the ways that I
have needed.

YESTER YEARS

You were always there to wipe and dry all my tears.
-M. Parris

Only yesterday I ran to you for everything: when there were monsters under my bed, a bobe on my elbow, when someone hurt my feelings and when all the problems that I thought were so big terrified me. You were there when I first started crawling, took my first step, my first fall, experienced my first upset, my first heartbreak. And you were always there to wipe and dry all my tears. You were there on my first day of elementary school, and now I'm ending high school. Remember when I climbed on top of the chair 'cause I thought that I could fly? Remember when I fell and broke my arm?

Remember when I won a bicycle for selling the most gift wrap? Remember when I learned how to read? Remember when I was a safety patroler? Remember when I came home from afterschool care all by myself? Remember when I didn't want to take my senior picture? Remember how it came out just fine? Remember when Healy had to go with me to get my stitches taken out and to my college auditions? Remember when I sneaked Lorenzo into the house? I remember when I thought I was in love....

These were all my yesteryears, so hold these memories dear and close to you. For in a blink they will be gone.

Monique Parris is a senior and drama major who will be attending Lees-McRae College in North Carolina in the fall of 2002. She has been writing since she was in the second grade. She won the poetry award for her poem, "They'll

See," in middle school, and she hasn't stopped writing since. "You write your first draft without your pen or pencil leaving the page. Then you go back and make it sound the way you want it to," she says.

THE BEAUTY OF HOPE
By Erica Naess

"Kindness springs from the soul of the individual."

I have given it my all.
But was treated unfairly
Yet I press on,
For that is the character of justice.
I have opened my heart
But was broken in return
Yet I press on,
For that is the nature of love.
I have shared my dreams
But was repressed
Yet I press on,
For that is the spirit of freedom.
I have cried puddles and rivers and oceans of salty tears
But was ignored,
Yet I press harder onward
For that is the beauty of hope.

Erica Naess, eighteen, will be attending the University of Florida in the fall of 2002. There she will study journalism and telecommunications for a year before moving to Southern California to pursue a career in the entertainment industry.

SECTION NINE

Candlelights of Kindness and Self-Control

Meet The Authors
L to R - Row 1: Jennifer Gonzalez, Felisha Croker,
Mayleen Ramirez. Row 2: Mike Baugh, Rafael Sanchez,
Sonya Cherres, Armand Valdes.

ENDOPLASM FUNK
By Sonya Cherres

This world is a splendor in itself for it is all we know.
-S. Cherres

An **endoplasm** rises from the darkness to project before
    our eyes,
A vision of a nautical deep beauty,
Blue and covered with lives,
We bit into creation with our incisor,
    This Tooth captivating humanity,
And cause corruption and antagonism in an oblivion that was
covered in peace.
    We've disturbed the ocean,
Our bare bodies are laved in the salt,
And in the flesh of the fish,
And we have stopped the silence with our palaver and
    powerful songs,
    Meaning nothing in the end
But deep empty souls,
The blurry water dissimulates our faces,
    And we hide existence beneath the waves,
Coaxed by a nostalgia that we dare not comprehend.
    The ocean is lacking peace,
We tossed our sin and treacheries thinking it will dissipate
    with the tide,
    And we hide but it remains,
Lingering in the thoughts that lie,
And lay
Upon the sand

Releasing our hands.
   The **ocean** has no patterns, no silk, nor gingham ties,
It has no reason to watch our fastidious eyes,
For it has been disturbed,
And when the sun sets into darkness,
And it is time for vespers in our pew,
We have become victims of sacrilege contentment,
   We follow ideology,
Smell the **funk**?
   The ocean is our herald to the past uniting all,
I'm just a baby,
     Telling me secrets?
   I cannot listen,
We are too concerned with nuances,
But we disturb you ocean nonetheless,
   This world is not a gim-crack,
It is a splendor in itself for it is all we know,
And in its relics we ignore the pain,
   And dump our oils and pollution,
And irrevocably, indefinitely the ocean is disturbed,
In our "visions" our endoplasm's that rise with the sun.

IDLE AFTERNOON
By Sonya Cherres

*"Kindness teaches us to understand and accept the truism
that life is a mystery to be lived."*

   Sit the female in
   Her body like an eggshell,
   Manipulation, Denunciation,
   She establishes "may I beg your pardon?"
   With a whisper of fear, not stated,
   She might not be encouraged,
   And then again it doesn't matter,

For he served her spirit on the platter,
He is nothing, As is she,
So let it be.

Collapse back on your recollections
And do nothing else.
Like a hard-boiled egg's so difficult to peel,
Wait...the story's easy to forget...
Her skin is taken off in pieces
She was not ready yet...

And she peels away the moment,
And she peels away the wound,
And she laughs at what's forgotten,
On one idle afternoon.

Hearts, blemished, indistinct,
Spurting like the valid sun,
She turns to hear him speaking,
But is left without anyone,
The arms of soldiers and of prophets,
Are not gentle enough you see
Because an eggshell is a weakling,
Therefore...let her be.
She is far more fragile than the broken glass,
Alas! She will not abide in it.

Yearning hearts into their arms and shoulders,
Are taking but a risk?
Because his arms are far too brisk,
They break her.

But a woman is more cherished.
She hides herself in boiling water.
Beneath shirts and heavy cologne

In order to bestow him ecstasy...
Still, when she unwraps the abnormal unsigned note
She let herself believe that it's from him.

And she tears away the letters,
Because they're leaving such a wound,
From something once forgotten,
On some idle afternoon.

Sonya Cherres is a senior who will be attending Florida International University in the fall of 2002. She hopes to live a life filled with happiness and health, surrounded by the people she loves. She hopes to fill others' lives with happiness, as well.

CANDLELIGHTS SCRIPT
By Mike Baugh

Setting: in a small and plain room, that seems comfortable, talking to an old friend

RICKY

I always loved doing things my way. It's been that way since (pause) I don't know. But I remember growing up and being hated most of my young life because I was very arrogant, and I didn't care much for anyone else. I mean, I used to be kind and courteous long ago, but I got nothing out of it. *(pause, shakes head slowly)*
As I got older my own selfishness and carelessness for others grew even worse. Some of my close friends have left me because of this. Even some of my life is a blur-maybe it's because I have been trying to block out so many bad situations, so many memories that have clogged my mind.
I don't know how all of this began. I only know that this attitude problem got worse and I couldn't control it. *(pause)* Just yesterday, for some strange reason, I wasn't feeling my usual self, and I was walking into a store when I saw an elderly couple struggling with their older daughter or something-the daughter must have been over thirty. Anyway, she was walking ahead of the couple, and the elderly guy trips—but, get this—she doesn't even look back.She acts as if she hears nothing. So, instinctively, I help the guy up, and he smiles at me, with a type of smile that I have never seen nor felt before, and I felt a tingling sensation in my chest. *(pauses to reflect as he looks up)* That unforgettable smile. And he patted me on the back. He didn't say thank you. I guess he didn't have

to. *(drops head, and picks it up as if coming to a realization)* Maybe—maybe part of my problem was ... was that I was looking for something in return for my good deeds, when I shouldn't have. Why, in this moment of time-why did I come to this realization at this time in my life? I'm a young man and I am just coming to this. You know I'm kind of glad this happened. At least I learned something about life and what it has to teach. "The goodness should come from your heart," my friends used to say, and I guess they were right.

Mike Baugh, a sophomore, says that he "loves to perform and take part in many productions," and he is more than willing "to lend a helping hand to others." In the future he plans to become an actor or be somehow involved in the performing arts field.

ON THE BUS
By Armand Valdes

*Now (following the terrorists' attacks), more than ever,
we have been seeing acts of kindness that have never
been seen before. -A. Valdes*

One of the things I've had to do most of my high school
career is ride the Metro bus. Since I don't yet have a car, the
bus has been my only means of transportation for a while.
Whenever my mom would be too busy at work to come pick
me up or I just didn't want to wait so long, this transportation
has been available. I think I rode the Coral Reef Max every
day for the last half of my freshman year and the majority of
my sophomore year. That's a lot of days.

Riding on the Max is an interesting experience. I have
learned many things about life and how things work. As a
writer, I have a knack for observing these things. For one, I
learned how to get around South Florida on $1.25. I also
learned a lot about human nature and how people function.

You couldn't imagine the types of people I have seen walk
through the bus doors. There are certain types of people I
like to call "sitters." (No, not for the obvious reason that they
sit on the bus!) Sitters come in and just carelessly sit around
as if they don't even care where the bus is going, just as long
as there are air conditioning and comfortable seats. These
are the people whom I really admire because they seem to
simply enjoy life. They sit down with smiles on their faces
and start conversations with the bus driver. These types of
people float through life enjoying the moments they have on
this earth. I sometimes sit there and admire them, wondering

who they are or where they are from.

Most of the people who use the buses aren't as carefree. They just sit down quietly 'til their stop comes and they get off. I could probably be classified in this group because I'm usually too tired to do much else besides stare out in front of me 'til I get off at my stop. There are other categories of riders, too, but other lessons are taught on bus rides. For one, I learned on the bus that life is not fair. For instance, if I am not standing precisely at the bus stop and ready to get on, even though I truly may want to catch the bus and am trying to get into position, the bus will never stop for me. I'm running on their schedule.

Much like life, people are not fair, either. There was one time I remember vividly. It was a Saturday afternoon and I was trying to get to the mall. It was really hot outside, and I was so happy to get under the air conditioning and lay back on the cushioned seats. The bus driver was an African American woman, kind of skinny and tall. We came to a stop and I saw a woman with about four children and an older lady. The younger woman got on and started speaking in Spanish to the bus driver, asking her a question. I couldn't understand because I don't speak Spanish and, apparently, neither did the bus driver. The bus driver interrupted her and said, "Listen lady, I live in America and I don't know no Spanish. I don't understand a word you're saying."

I thought at that moment about how awkward that was for everyone. The children and the old woman were still outside in the blistering heat, and they were eager to get on. Then the woman began to speak in very weak English. "Does dis bus go to, eh, Dadelan' Sout'? We need to get on de 96 bus."

Now, I knew very well that this bus was the Max, not the 96, but I also knew that it did go to Dadeland South. Surely the women and children could get on the bus to go there. I opened my mouth to say something, but I was interrupted by the driver. "You wait here and the next bus will come in a few minutes." The woman's children were becoming restless and the old woman was holding one in her arms. The younger woman flashed a smile and said, "Oh, t'ank you. We have been waiting here for two hours." I felt really bad for them. Two hours in that weather was not fun. We drove off and left them there in the heat like that.

I realized that day that people can, unfortunately, be unkind and hurtful to others, just because someone speaks another language or acts a different way. Was the bus driver justified in leaving the lady, her children and the old woman? I wonder.

Of course, the bus ride is not always a cruel world. Everyday someone performs an act of kindness on the bus. Every time someone gives up a seat to someone else-well, right there is a great act of kindness. Complete strangers and they treat other others like their own family. Now, you may say that this is simple courtesy, but is it? Just as easily as someone can move over or stand up to make room for another rider, couldn't they also just put their bag down in the seat besides them and spare themselves the company, or otherwise ignore the person standing?

This is a great show of human nature to be kind to others when others need help. Sure, it's not as drastic as what some public servants do, who go out each night, risking their lives, so that we can enjoy ours. Nor is it more important than someone picking up something someone else dropped. On one level or another, all these acts add up and are equally important.

Now, more than ever, we have been seeing acts of kindness that have never been seen before. I'm proud to say that there are people in New York City right now who are helping clean up Ground Zero and restore the confidence of our nation, while I am scooting over a few inches to allow an exhausted person to sit down in comfort.

Riding the bus has taught me many things. Not only has

it given me a great sense of direction but also a life lesson that will stick with me forever. When I ride the bus and take a look at the people around me, I wonder about their lives and whether they see what I see. I hope you do.

Armand Valdes, a Critic's Choice playwright, is a sophomore. His play, "How to Beat Everyone Else in Monopoly," will be performed this summer by the City Theatre. He wants "to thank everyone who is helping the fight against discrimination."

STAR

By Jennifer Gonzalez

I would rather be a star

I am not a well-known shape
Shining in the sky

I can't sparkle from a distance
Across the corners of the world

I am not well lit
I am no great metaphor for wishes
I am not among other stars

I stand completely alone
I do not have my own song.

I would have a magic touch
Children would wish upon me

As the night falls
I would provide light for lovers
Standing beneath me

I would be visible for all to see
Through their windows
I would be the glitter to the sky

I would be the added beauty...
A candlelight of kindness
And self-control
For the whole world to admire.

TO LIVE
By Jennifer Gonzalez

To live is to share success while giving back to the world.
-J. Gonzalez

(To live) is to dream.
To dance on the moon,
Run barefoot in the park,
To play freely
    in the rain while
Singing through the wind,
Counting confident stars,
And watching slowly passing clouds fade

(To live) is to love unconditionally
To appreciate the gift of friendship
And return it happily.
To love and be loved back
To see more than what you're looking at
To love more and hate less
To smile longer and not frown
To spread sunshine and joy wherever you go
While saying a word of encouragement
To someone who is feeling blue.

(To live) is to have self-confidence
To know that experiencing hardships only strengthens you
And that there are more good times than there will be bad.
To stand up for what you believe in and know something
    better lies ahead
To sacrifice and understand the sacrifices of others
To allow yourself to take risks and make mistakes
As long as you learn from them and rather than running
    from fears, face them.

(To live) is to live life to its fullest
To indulge in life's ecstasies and stop to smell the flowers
To know the best things in life are free
And that there is no limit to happiness
For life is what you make it.
To watch the sun set and rise and not be afraid
    to chase rainbows
To share success while giving back to the world
To persevere and believe in yourself
To commit to never give up and to give
    and not expect in return
And have the chance to witness miracles.

(To die) is to wake up
To give in to prejudice,
To breathe in hatred and consume violence while giving up
    on hopes and dreams.
To attack a spirit of kindness because of self-insecurities
And not take advantage of flowing opportunities
To judge unfairly and discriminate against
To be closed-minded while going through life bitter
Instead of changing the world.

(To die) is to wake up or live life without dreaming.

Jennifer Gonzalez is a high schooler who loves to write poetry that projects her thoughts and feelings. Her favorite hobby is reading. Jennifer enjoys family, friends and school.

DANCE
By Rafael Sanchez

A dancer is only as good as her music... she cannot perform well unless she feels the rhythm in her body. -R. Sanchez

Lila and her mother sat in the living room of her grandmother's spacious, two-bedroom apartment. Lila was three years old. Her grandmother pushed a tape into the VCR and hit play.

"This is my favorite dance out of all the dances I've ever seen, sweetie."

The television screen was flooded with black and white snow until the image of a single girl on stage appeared. A thin, beautiful girl with long, black, shining hair took the stage and filled the auditorium with her presence.

"Nana!" That's you!" Lila screamed. Her grandmother nodded and asked if Lila recognized that song. The familiar rhythm and tune brought a smile to Lila's face. It was the melody of a deep Indian song accompanied by the booming of drums and hums of flutes. "Moon Song."

"That's my bedtime song!" Lila remembered that she was part Seminole and that her grandmother would sing her to sleep with that very song. When her grandmother was eighteen, she had performed a dance to her own bedtime song, which her mother sang to her.

The familiar intro jolted her from her memories and sped her heart rate as she finished her stretching. Lila got to her feet and took her position, for the dance class was about to begin. It was sixth period, and she realized that after school she would have to drive to her studio to dance for three more hours. Lila loved to dance. Her grandmother had been a Broadway dancer and had convinced Lila's father to let her get into dance classes when she was three years old. Her grandmother paid for the classes and, even though it was a lot of money for competitions and costumes, she thought it was worth it to see her beautiful granddaughter follow in her footsteps.

The dance class commenced as the group began to move in unison. Lila moved easily through the air while many in the class struggled to lift themselves into the proscribed jump. Most of the girls ran off to the sides, symbolizing their going off stage, and left Lila, Monique and Sara to perform their trio. The girls got into formation and with the music's growing intensity, spun into faster and faster fouettés and jumped out into the air. Moving by muscle memory and not thinking about the dance, Lila thought, instead, of how high she had seen her grandmother jump in the old films. She wanted to be just like her, and knowing how much money her dance lessons were costing grandma, she tried her best to never miss a class.

When they moved on to the solo pieces, Lila refocused her attention. The show would take place in a month and rehearsals started after school on the following Monday. It was Friday, so all the girls were excited about going out with their boyfriends or seeing a movie. All except Lila, who loved to go to an empty dance room and practice. It kept her in shape and practice always makes perfect, she knew.

Lila had three solo pieces choreographed but couldn't decide which one she wanted to perform. They were all great pieces, and she worked very hard on them in private session with her teachers. She performed them all for the class and her peers loved each one, but Lila just didn't think any of them were right. She knew that there was only one person who could help her out. Nana.

She found time to go see her grandmother every Saturday afternoon after her morning session at the studio. Lila spent more time with her than with her mother. Lila's grandmother was one of the major influences in her life, and she didn't know what she would do without her. She loved her with all her soul, and she couldn't imagine dancing without her Nana there to see it.

It was the week of the show when she finally decided to ask her grandmother's advice. Her grandmother had seen all the dances and thought they were all marvelous. "Nana, the thing is...I'm just not feeling it-you know?" Her grandmother nodded and explained that a dancer is only as good as her music; that she cannot perform well unless she feels the rhythm in her body. Lila considered that maybe her music was the problem. She just didn't know. All the dances were about the same length, so her spot in the show would be kept open unless she couldn't figure it out by the following Wednesday.

"Lila, dear, I love you on stage. You are a beautiful dancer and I know whatever you choose, it will be ..." Her sentence was broken with a sudden cough.

"Nana? Are you okay?" Lila asked. Her grandmother tried to shake her head as her hands came to her throat. Her voice came in short, raspy breaths. "Nana? Nana? What's wrong?" Lila screamed as her grandmother collapsed on the floor.

In the hours to come, Nana was hospitalized. Tubes, needles and monitors were connected and beeped and buzzed around her. Lila sat at her bedside holding on to her grandmother's hand, as if holding her to this world. It was 3:00 AM that Sunday morning when her grandmother nudged Lila from her dreams. "Lila...what were we talking about, sweetie? You know, before I collapsed like some old woman..." she said with a grin.

With tears in her eyes, Lila spoke with a trembling voice. "Are you okay, Nana? You scared me so much! Please tell me you're okay."

"Calm down, sweetie," she began. "I'm fine...I'm fine."

"Are you sure?" Her grandmother nodded, "Nana, I still don't know what to do. The performance is this week, and I still don't know what dance to do!"

"Just follow your heart and everything will be answered. Look deep into your heart and what you find there will inspire you for the right dance. Dance comes from the heart. If you have heart, you can't lose.... I'm a little tired, baby, I'm going to take a nap. You should do the same. When I get out of this crazy place, we're gonna dance our feet to the bone!"

"I love you, Nana."

"I'll love you forever, sweetie. Never forget that ..." And as she fell asleep, she stroked Lila's hand and hummed the "Moon Song."

Just then, Lila's mother came and told her to come home. Lila refused, but her mother forced her to leave. Lila kissed her grandmother on the forehead before she left. After she got home, she continued humming the" Moon Song" until she fell asleep.

Later that afternoon, Lila woke up hearing people moving downstairs. She stretched and climbed out of bed to see who was down there. She descended the stairs and in the living room she saw her mother and father, her uncle and her two aunts. They were all crying. Lila instantly knew what had happened. "No...no..." she repeated, as her mother approached her with tear-soaked cheeks.

"No! No! She's not dead! Please! NO!" Lila collapsed to the floor and wept. Her mom knelt beside her and wrapped her arms around her. They both wailed with sorrow.

It was the night of the show. The previous days had passed so very slowly, ever since her grandma had died. Without her Nana, Lila thought dance was hollow. Empty, like her heart. Before she took the stage for her solo, Lila picked up the microphone.

"Thank you all for being here tonight. We've worked

long and hard to bring you this show. And for all those who can't be here tonight...we wish you..." Her voice cracked as she fought back the tears. "...We wish you were...and it's not the same without you...I hope you all enjoy this tribute to a very important person in my life who couldn't be here with us." She took her position and as the familiar rhythms of the "Moon Song" pulsated through the auditorium, Lila wiped a tear from her cheek and began her tribute to her Nana.

Rafael Sanchez is a freshman enrolled in the Visual and Performing Arts Academy. He enjoys every aspect of the visual and performing arts and hopes to eventually attend college and become a professional performer.

REACTION TO "DEARLY DEPARTED"
By Derek Sutta

"The art of success is discovering the best talents, skills and abilities and applying them where they will make the most effective contribution to your fellow men."

"Dearly Departed" was beyond anything I expected. I was afraid of anyone missing his or her lines or cues. The cast was amazing! When the lights went up, everything fell into place. The worries left my mind right after my scene in the kitchen with "my wife." Honestly, I felt like I was acting during that scene, but everyone tells me that scene was great, that it seemed entirely "natural." I guess that I was just thinking about it. By the eighth scene (the one with "Junior" and me), I was completely in character and I had forgotten about the audience. Forgetting about the audience was one of my goals when we spoke about what was on our minds before we went onstage. Before the play, we did our warm-ups, which lacked energy, and which I didn't like. Yet, everyone had such an amazing adrenaline rush that warm-ups didn't even matter. I understand that in the morning when everyone is tired you need great, energetic warm-ups; but it was nighttime.

The coolest part was being treated as though you were famous. The crew really treats you well. If you are missing a prop, you don't even have to lift a finger; they will get it for you. That fact was amazing to me. I had come straight from middle school plays where I did everything: I wrote, directed, ran the lights and sound, and acted in every production at school. Also the wardrobe and makeup crew was beyond

238 / Alice Johnson

anything that I thought would be in our production. When I heard I had to wear makeup, I thought it was a joke. But it wasn't and I really felt important when I had somebody putting it on me.

When I went home, my parents told me that they loved the play. They then told me, "You were good, but Guermillo was the best." I just sat there thinking: well, at least they didn't lie. My little brother backed them up, so did everyone else with whom I talked. So, all I have to say to their comments is, "Good job, Guermillo."

The next day in school, I had people whom I have never seen walking up to me and telling me that I was great in the play! In fact, so many people told me I was good in that play that I got tired of saying, "Thank you." The most common question was: "Why didn't you go for drama?" I just said, "Yeah." I am still kind of disappointed that I didn't get in, but I would never have thought that I would see the stage in my business days at Coral Reef.

Mr. Battle was great. I hadn't acted in two years; he brought back a great deal of the skills that were rusty. He would show me what he was seeing in the scene; with his excellent acting skills it was very easy to see what he wanted. The scene with "Clyde" was the most Battle-influenced. We stayed after school one day until about five o'clock and I threw that scene together. The outcome was amazing. Jeremy did an excellent job of portraying the gay man, and I didn't laugh so that made me happy. I knew I was in character so I was rather confident that I would laugh. Mr. Battle wrote every single person in the cast a personal letter. That was exactly the confidence boost that I needed in order to go out on stage and perform the way that I knew I could without having an extreme case of bad nerves.

From this play, I have decided to join Thespians, our Coral Reef High School theatre group. I really would love to compete in a drama competition. From there I will decide how good I really am in this field and decide whether to pursue it further as a career. I was able to act with kids in the "Drama Stand" and they said that they would love to do a "Thespian" competition with me. That was a really great thing to hear.

The play was great, I am just sad that it is over. I know that we are probably going to go into theatre history and that doesn't excite me, but you never know how good it might be. Overall, it was a great experience that I will never forget.

Derek Sutta is a student in the International Baccalaureate theatre program at Coral Reef Senior High School. Obviously, his interests and pursuits are wide and varied.

THE CALL
By Felisha Croker

The events described took place during my last year of middle school. However, all names, except my own, have been changed.

Countdown! 10...9...8...7...6...5...4...3...2...1! The last day of school!

"So, Felisha, it's the last day of school. What ya gonna do?" my friend Dania says.

"I'm going to Disney World!! No, I'm just kidding." I always play around.

"Kiara, what's wrong?" I say. Kiara was crying lakes.

"We're never coming back to this ghetto school again!"

So I took her camera and took a picture of the school. "Here, now when you look at this picture, you can pretend that you are there." I tried to make her stop crying.

"Thanks, girl," she replied.

About twenty minutes later I return home. "Hey, I'm home," I announce to no one in particular. I run right to my room and think of him. Trayvon McKenzie. I liked him for two years. We were really good friends. Yet, he didn't come on the last day of school. I wonder if he might have been sick or something. Yeah, that's it, I think. He was sick.

And no more school until August 27th. So what am I gonna do? All I usually do is watch TV.

It's the next day with nothing to do. But I hear the doorbell ring and I wonder who it is. I run to answer it.

"Hey, what's up, girl! What you doing here?" My friends

Dania and her sister Dakia have stopped by.

"We don't want to stay long, but what are you doing now, Felisha?" Dania asks.

"Nothing, why?"

"You want to go swimming?"

"Dania, where are we going to go swimming?" At first I didn't really want to go.

"Felisha, I told you...at my house!"

"Wait, you got a pool?"

"Yeah!"

"Okay, hold up, I got to go ask my dad." I go to dad and ask, "Dad, can I go swimming at Dania's house?"

"Felisha, Dania's got a pool?!" My dad says, sounding astonished.

"Yeah, I just figured that out."

"Well, okay. But give me their phone number so I can call them to have you come home later."

"Okay!" I give him Dania's phone number, get all my stuff ready, then get my bike and am ready to go.

Two hours pass and I am in the pool, my hair is wet and my fingers look like ten small prunes. "Hey, Dania, is Trayvon coming?" I ask.

"Nah, he ain't coming."

"Why?"

"Nothing, Dania. Nothing."

"Hey! You like Trayvon!! Ewww!" she acts like she was surprised. I told her how I felt four days earlier. I guess she wasn't listening. She never does.

"You know what I heard, Felisha?"

"What did you hear, Dania?" She really thought I wanted to know. And she was right.

"He's moving."

"He who?"

"Trayvon."

"Oh, my God! I never had the chance to tell him!" I felt like crying a river.

"See!! You do like him!"

"So, shutup, Dania!"   The phone rings and Dakia rushes to pick it up.

"Hello? Who? Oh." And shouting to me, she says, "Felisha, it's for you."

"Who is it-my dad?" I ask.

"Naw. Who is this?" she echoes to the caller. After a pause she continues, happily, "Felisha, it's Trayvon!"

I run right out of the pool like there is a roach in the water. "Hey, Trayvon."

"Hey, girl."

"Where were you yesterday? Huh? It was the last day of school! Why weren't you there?" I asked him all these questions quickly. After all, I really did like him.

"Dang, girl, you're going so fast. I guess you heard."

"Heard what?" I answered as though I knew what he meant.

"I'm moving."

"Where are you moving?"

"Back to New York."

"Why, Trayvon? Why!?" I was so mad, I felt like hitting someone.

"Dang, girl, why you so...so...so..." he didn't know what to say, so I said if for him.

"I care for you?"

"Yeah. That." He's a really stupid child. Ha!

"When are you leaving?"

"I'm leaving in two days."

"Trayvon, I might never see you again!" I can't really see him because I won't be allowed to go out with boys until I'm sixteen. Boys can't really come to my house that much, either.

"Well...Felisha, I wanted to say that I like you. A lot. A

lot."

When he said that, I felt like fainting. "Trayvon, I like you too." I wanted to tell the whole world!

"Ooo, what are we gonna do?"

"Trayvon, I don't know." I wanted to cry.

"Well, this is probably the last time I could really talk to you."

"What about the next two days?" I asked.

"I'm going to pack and my parents have to cut off the phones."

"So, is this good bye?"

"If you want to call it that, girl."

"Well, bye, Trayvon. I'll think of you everyday. Okay?"

"Okay, Felisha...bye."

My heart sank like the Titanic as I hung up the phone.

"Ohhh, girl! So what happened?" Dania asked.

"Dania, something I will never forget."

Although we did not have much time to build a relationship, I was grateful for the chance to meet a boy I liked a lot, who also liked me.

Felisha Croker, fifteen, would like to pursue an entertainment career—whether as an actress, a singer or a professional basketball player. Among her favorite spare time activities are acting, singing or playing basketball, she says, as well as "hanging out with my friends."

THE FLIP SIDE OF HILARITY
By Mayleen Ramirez

*"Kindness helps us to meet the challenges of life
with the art of laughter."*

I love to laugh. There is nothing else in the world that makes me happier than when I laugh. Laughing is a relaxation exercise to me. It soothes my inner soul and releases all of my stress. I am not embarrassed when I laugh. The only problem is when I laugh too hard.

One day at school in my theatre class, my friend and I were listening to another day's worth of boring lectures about theatre history. I was cracking up, I just could not stop, and I would laugh at the simplest things. After a hard, long stare that I received from the teacher, I decided to calm down. So I took my water bottle out from my purse to take a sip. Then my friend sitting next to me whispered a phrase, an inside joke we share, and I just couldn't help it—I burst out laughing and sprayed the person in front of me with water that was still in my mouth. Well, because of what happened to me, my friend started laughing uncontrollably, as well.

The student in front me was wearing a sweater at the time, and he quickly wiped the water off, took off the sweater and stuffed it in his backpack. I hope he washed it when he got home. I ran to the bathroom to get toilet paper to help dry off everyone else I accidentally sprayed.

That day I learned to leave the laughing outside of my classes and concentrate more on the teachers and the lessons. Even so, this was the most embarrassing, yet hilarious moment my friend and I had ever experienced.

Mayleen Ramirez is a freshman enrolled in the theatre magnet program. She loves "to draw costume renderings for plays" and hopes to eventually become a costume designer.

KINDNESS CAN BE A MAGNET
By David Solomon

There was a boy named Jack
And a girl named Jill
She really didn't want to go up the hill.

Her parents told her just be nice
And maybe, just maybe, have the time of her life,
Someday, maybe, even be his wife.

Jack was thrilled to hear such good news.
It made his day, week and month, too.
If kindness is done, it returns back to you.

You see, Jack had done favors for Jill for a while. He had gone out of his way to be kind and encouraging. He wanted to be her friend, but she was reluctant to respond. Once she decided it would be okay to get to know him, she found he was a great person and a fun friend. He was very glad to finally get to know Jill, and it was his kindness that helped make this possible.

David Solomon is involved in the drama program and enjoys acting and working with lighting design. He is actively involved in the community and is a Boy Scout. He also works as a lifeguard.

FCAT
Anonymous

Laughter is the best medicine, especially for us foreigners.

Here in Miami, Florida, we have over sixty nationalities of us foreigners who are trying hard to learn how to speak the English language in order that we might score much higher on the FLORIDA COMPREHENSIVE ASSESSMENT TEST (FCAT). In my opinion, I feel that many native Americans do not realize how difficult the English language actually is. Take for instance, the following poem which I now quote, on behalf of my fellow classmates.

Where can a man buy a **cap** for his **knee**, (**kneecap?**)
Or a key to the **lock of his hair**?
Can his **eyes** be called an **academy**
Because there are **pupils** there?

On the **crown of his head**, what gems are found?
Who travels **the bridge of his nose**?
Can he use in shingling the roof of his house
The **nails on the end of his toes**?

Can the **crook of his elbow** be sent jail?
If so, what did it do?
How can he sharpen his **shoulder blade**?
I'll be hanged if I know! Do you?

Can he sit in the shade of **the palm in his hand**,
Or beat on the **drum of his ear**?
Can the **calf on his leg** eat the **corn on his toe**?
If so, why not grow corn on the ear?

Coral Reef Senior High School Authors

PART II

$\mathcal{C}$andlelights: The Silent Deeds of Kindness

Next to the home and the church, schools are the greatest influence in the development of personality and character.
—The National Education Association

KINDNESS IS A CRSH PROJECT

"Fill the Void Newsletter"

Teach each child to ask himself: Is the world a better place because of me? —*The National Education Association*

I was greatly impressed by an outstanding document from Coral Reef Senior school students entitled *Fill the Void Newsletter* because it is the epitome of what kindness is all about. *Fill the Void* is the name of a charitable activity sponsored by the students at Coral Reef Senior High School. Because the activities are so astounding and the project is an event practically every high school in the world would be interested in initiating (if not already involved in such a project), I asked permission to print the entire newsletter.

Alice W. Johnson, Editor, Candlelights Series

Fill The Void Newsletter

National Volunteer Week-
by Priyanka Handa, Sergeant-at-Arms

National volunteer week not only honors volunteers but also highlights their contribution and necessity to the community. The week of April 22nd brought various festivities in acknowledgment of the countless hours of self-service, to which Fill the Void contributed greatly as an integral part of organizations dedicated to serving the Miami-Dade Community. Looking back at the activities that the club participated in, we are proud to include the Coconut Grove Art Festival, Camillus House, Habitat for Humanity and adopting needy families during the holiday season, among many others. This year's accomplishments for the club have motivated and encouraged an increase in the student body's participation towards the advancement of their community. Our goal is to continue dedicating our time to help others and encourage participation in the club. Remember that the larger the magnitude of our members, the greater the impact of our community!

Future Plans: Fill the Void Activities 2002-2003
By Katie Vila, Secretary

This year is coming to an end and Fill the Void is beginning to consider possible projects for the upcoming school year. As most of you know the club has participated in various successful activities this year and would like to continue this trend by enhancing our participation in community service as well as diversifying the projects that we are involved in. A few of our members have begun to submit suggestions for the 2002-2003 school year. "I think that it would be an interesting experience to collect toys for children and deliver them to hospitals or orphanages during the holiday season," said Nick Alves, a current member. Other members including Blanca Cuero suggested continuing the adopt-a-family project throughout the year and not limiting it to the holiday season. Keeping CAS projects in mind, IB junior Lara Bueso suggested that "it would be wonderful if the club could take part in [her] project which is dedicated to providing less fortunate schools with necessary supplies." All of the ideas suggested are great. The club will try to incorporate all of them in the following year's activities.

KINDNESS IS SHARING

*A RECIPE FOR THE SUCCESSFUL SENIOR HIGH
SCHOOL STUDENT*

8 Cups of HAVING A GOAL
8 Cups of SELF-RESPECT
4 Cups of COMMITMENT
4 Tablespoons of CONFIDENCE
4 Ounces of SACRIFICES
4 Teaspoons of COOPERATION
6 Teaspoons of FORTITUDE
4 Cups of the WILL TO SUCCEED
1 Barrel of DESIRE TO GRADUATE

Take your Goals, Commitment and Self-Respect, mix
generously with Confidence and the Will to Succeed. Sprinkle
liberally with Cooperation and Fortitude. Blend in Sacrifices.
Garnish with the Desire to Graduate. If you follow this recipe
carefully, YOU will attain the necessary skills to be a
SUCCESSFUL GRADUATE!
        —Compliments of the CRSH School of Culinary Arts

KINDNESS IS SHARING

CRSH CLASS NOTES

"FOLLOWING IN THE FAMILY FOOTSTEPS"
(An excerpt from The South Dade Newsleader
A Community Newspaper—*8/20/2001)*

Edwina Bullard, daughter of State Representative Edward and Larcenia Bullard, is entering her senior year at Coral Reef High with honor, grace and responsibility. She was *recently elected Student Government President by her peers. She won the election after facing her opponent in a run-off.*

Coral Reef serves a diverse student population with a total of five academies. They are Agriscience, Leisure Medicine, *Legal and Public Affairs, Business and Finance and Performing Arts. It is listed as the largest of magnet schools in the nation. The students take pride in the school and boasts great school spirit.*

Edwina is a member of the Marching Band and Health Occupation Students of America. She cares about the people *in the school setting— both adults and peers.* She was very *excited to take part in student politics.*

"I was pretty much excited about the election," said Edwina. "My mom and my dad have been in politics since I *was in kindergarten. I said to myself in ninth grade that I would run for student government. I ran in the tenth grade for Secretary of Student Government, but lost.*

"I ran recently and won election to be Student Government President," she added. "I originally had eight opponents, so there had to be a run-off election since no one received 50%

the first time. I won the run-off election against a classmate of mine. It was a clean campaign. I am proud to say that I am the first African-American female to be elected Student Government President at Coral Reef Senior High. Also, it is the first time that both the Student Government President and the Student Government Vice-President have been females serving at the same time. The Student Government Vice-President is Ashley Boxer."

Edwina attended West Laboratory Elementary and Southwood Middle and maintained honor role status. She has been on the regular honor roll as well as the principal's honor roll. She earned numerous awards during her eleven years in the Miami-Dade Public School System and now as a senior, she has received a Letter of Commendation from the National Honor Roll recognizing her outstanding academic performance, and has been selected for induction into the 2001-2002 National Honor Society.

Edwina's accomplishments will be showcased. The achievement offers her an opportunity to be awarded scholarships annually administered by the Educational Research Center of America. Her biography will be published in high school libraries, colleges and universities nationwide. She has reached a level of accomplishment shared by only 4.5 percent of all United States high school students.

KINDNESS IS SHARING

TEN STRATEGIES FOR HEALING UNKIND MOMENTS
by Edwina Bullard, Student Government President

A gift of leadership is an obligation to lead. -NEA Journal

We certainly appreciate the kindnesses of our parents and teachers who are guiding our growth by being role models of good leadership. From them we learn that if we wish to cultivate an attitude of kindness so that we can be at peace with ourselves and with others, we need to learn how to control our anger. Based on their teachings, the following are ten behavior patterns that I have compiled to share with you for those moments when you feel unkind:

1. BE AWARE OF THE SIGNALS, your signals and the other person's (perhaps your schoolmate's) signals. Maybe your schoolmate is tired. Is he/she disappointed? Sick? Depressed? Feels isolated? Lonely? Unloved? Feels detached? You might avoid trouble by studying these attitudes.
2. ASK YOURSELF, "AM I ACTING OR REACTING?" Am I losing my temper because my classmate has lost his/hers? This is an excellent question to ask yourself. Oftentimes this is called "hooking my child." Ask yourself, "Will I go down to her/his level of behavior or bring her/him up to mine? Remember the adage: "Don't let anyone drag you so low as to make you hate him."
3. REMEMBER, TIMING IS OF GREAT IMPOR-TANCE. Kindness lessons teach us that mature anger

has a long fuse. Actually, some things take care of themselves when we delay action. Should things become worse, just remember that a postponed response is usually better.

4. IF YOU CAN TRUTHFULLY AGREE SOMEWHERE IN THE DISAGREEMENT, START THERE. Remember, you can disagree without being disagreeable. You will win your points, more likely, if he/she knows you've seen his/hers. Always start with the assumption that your critics might be right.

5. SPEAK SOFTLY. In angry moments, a soft voice disarms your antagonist because it takes him/her by surprise.

6. AVOID SARCASM, RIDICULE, MIMICRY, SCORN, PESSIMISM. Remember, these attitudes never advance your cause because they are often a reflection of one's own weakness.

7. APOLOGY, LIKE KINDNESS, IS FOR THE GREAT PEOPLE. Learn to say "I'm sorry" with meaning. Let it come from the depths of the heart. Remember, anger has not been fully handled until it has expressed regrets with sincerity. Politeness is not only the most powerful but also the easiest argument.

8. PUT THE BEST, RATHER THAN THE WORST INTERPRETATION ON THE ACTS OF OTHERS. "Small minds discuss people, average minds discuss events, great minds discuss ideas."

9. IDEAS ARE DIAMONDS. Let us discuss the idea of transforming the world through deeds of kindness in our international war against hate and terrorism.

10. CULTIVATE AN ATTITUDE OF KINDNESS. Treat others as you would have them treat you. Don't you want to be treated with kindness, respect and compassion? Remember the traditional saying: When we cultivate an attitude of kindness, we can become too large for worry,

too noble for anger, too strong for fear and too happy to be submerged by trouble.

Kindness is Sharing

"MY COUNTRY"
by Junior Orange Bowl Queen Kelyn Rodriguez

My Country...what does it mean to me? To be sincere, I don't know what to say. I was born in Tegucigalpa, Honduras, a small country located in Central America. I came to the United States when I was eleven months old. I was born in a Spanish country, but raised in an all-American community.

My younger siblings were born here. "They are American, and you are Honduran," my parents always say. I understand them, but that's not how I feel. While my brother and sister consider themselves 100% American, I don't consider myself all Honduran because there is still a "gringo" side of me. I feel 50% American and 50% Honduran.

To me, "country" means a place where everyone is united for many reasons and enjoys such rights as freedom of religion, safety and other needs. Don't get me wrong and think I just like the U.S. more than Honduras. I only imply that the United States is a well-developed country, and it's the opposite of Honduras when talking about the economy. After Hurricane Mitch, Honduras has been struggling for ways to help everyone in the country by building new houses and giving food to the needy.

What matters most to me is the culture, such as the food, the nationality or the beauty of a country. Honduras has a lot of beautiful scenery, such as *Las Islas de la Bahia,* meaning the islands on the bay, bursting with exotic colors such as pink, red, yellow and orange. With lovely sunsets and warm, seashore breezes, it's a place where anyone would feel as if he/she were in paradise. On the other hand, Miami also has wonderful beaches and nice restaurants on the seashore.

I love *tamales*, the traditional Honduran food made of meat and vegetables such as peas, potatoes and rice, with hot sauce on top. I eat them on the most important holidays, like Christmas, Independence Day or New Year's Day. Although I love tamales, I can never say "No" to a chicken sandwich with french fries from Checkers or an ice cream sundae with hot fudge and peanuts from McDonalds.

After the September 11th tragedy, I thought, "Would I die for the U.S. or Honduras?" I came to the conclusion I would only die for my religion and family. I'm still proud of my Spanish background. Yet, I felt very patriotic wearing my Old Navy T-shirt with the U.S. flag printed on it. The names South America, Central America and North America mean nothing individually to me because we are all Americans.

PART III
Shared Wisdom from the High School Student's World

Judicious praise for worthy effort is one of the most important arts of the teacher.
—*The National Education Association*

ON LISTENING TO TOMORROW'S GENERATION

*Who dares to teach must never cease to learn. No teacher
can be his best as a teacher who is not himself teachable.*
—*NEA Journal*

As high school scholars eager to help fight the
international war on terrorism, and who dare to transform
their world through deeds of kindness, the students at Coral
Reef Senior High School have accepted the responsibility of
doing their part. Following the terrorists' attacks on September
11, 2001, these students, like millions of school students
throughout the universe, realized that the world needs
kindness. This is especially highlighted in seventeen-year-
old Chandler Griffith's story entitled *A Maze of Grace*. In
addition, our young authors like Chandler feel that every
individual needs to be awakened to the everyday acts of
kindness that embrace his/her world and express gratitude
for these spiritual thoughts, feelings and actions. This can
easily be done from the depths of the heart through gratitude
journal writing.

As noted in my introduction, while compiling and editing
the CRSH students' stories for this "Candlelights" volume,
we could not help but be drawn to tears, so touching were the
characters and situations the young authors described.
Consider fifteen-year-old Cristian Bossa's story entitled *A
Loving Child*. Stories like Cristan's revealed to us that children
are, indeed, great teachers, enabling us to see the innocent
child that still lives within us. When we take time to listen to
the children's voices, giving them praise when earned, they
can teach us grown-ups that kindness begins at home where
the fruits of the spirit should be practiced daily. The home
should be the center of kindness and compassion. Our sixteen-
year-old author, Dennis Barbato, gives us the perfect example
of this wisdom in his story entitled *Mother: Another Word*

for Kindness.

The students' personal stories reveal to us that next to the home and the church, the schools are the greatest influence in the development of personality and character. The children's writings also show us that, based on their own human experiences, kindness embraces all the other eight virtues. Relating human experiences, the students conveyed to us that by being kind, we have the power to make the world a happier place in which to live. Their stories tell us that by being kind to one another, we can help diminish the amount of fear, sorrow, despair and frustration, not only in the world of high school students, but throughout the universe. Many of their stories show us by human examples that the world is unkind only because of the lack of kindness in the individuals who live in it.

The young authors are telling us that there is no greater kindness than that which has its inspiration through love. An example of this insight can be found in fifteen-year-old Asha Hill's story, *An Act of Kindness*, where she describes how friends helped her adjust to her new home, Throughout this book, concerned high schoolers talk about human experiences that touch lives and lift spirits, and that cover a wide range of human emotions. In so doing, they highlight their thoughts and feelings that reflect the spiritual world of kindness. They share with the reader true and inspirational stories about people courageously performing deeds of kindness for others. As earlier stated, many of the stories are dramatic and emotional, enabling the reader to feel more grateful, compassionate, loving and more enlightened, awakened and alive with the spirit of kindness.

It is our hope that the stories will awaken you, our readers, to our human interconnectedness, interrelatedness and interdependence, enabling you to embrace the joy of feeling spiritually united as a child of the universe. Because kindness encompasses all the virtues, the CRSH authors focused the following nine virtues: (1) Love, (2) Joy, (3) Peace, (4) Patience, (5) Kindness, (6) Goodness, (7) Faithfulness, (8) Gentleness and (9) Self-Control. The nine virtues represent the ninth month of the year, September, the month of the terrorists' attacks. Each virtue has eleven stories each to represent the eleventh day of September. Thus we focus 9/11 with approximately 2001 hours of individual meditation.

When students meditate, they know that they are in communication with their higher selves. It was our fervent request that they cultivate the art of meditating before engaging in serious writing that flows from the heart and soul, the center of their true thoughts and feelings. Being students who are enrolled in Mrs. Ana Mederos's drama class, they were all familiar with speaking from the soul within themselves. As a result, they found it comfortable to share their thoughts and feelings on the subject of kindness, thus beautifully highlighting the purpose of the series.

LESSONS LEARNED FROM
THE CHILDREN'S STORIES

Teach children the highest values. –NEA Journal

Life teaches us all through human experiences that we attract what we give away. Thus, we know that when we give away acts of kindness, such as love, joy, peace, patience, goodness, faithfulness and gentleness, we bring these acts of kindness back into our own lives. We can bring more kindness into our lives by bringing more kindness into the lives of others. We can bring more joy into our lives by bringing more joy into the lives of others. We can bring more peace into our lives by bringing more peace into the lives of others. And the deeds of kindness go on an on, incorporating all the virtues.

Some of the young authors keep gratitude journals of their personal experiences. Basically, through gratitude journal writing, students are awakened to the universal law of cause and effect because they see and feel the joy of being grateful and the glorious mystery of why we attract what we give away. This insight is truly an awakening of the spirit, inasmuch as we are spiritual beings housed in human bodies. It awakens us to look deeply into our own lives and actually get to know our true selves—who are we, where are we going and why? Through gratitude journal writing, we discover that we thirst for certain personal needs to help us feel genuine fulfillment. We find that we are here to spread kindness because it is in spreading kindness that we feel genuine fulfillment. This truth is exemplified in many of the stories in this book.

Therefore, when we ask ourselves what do we need more of in our lives, we can reflect on the virtue of kindness because, as the young authors have taught us, it encompasses all of the other virtues. We can keep gratitude journals highlighting the acts of kindness we receive from others. If we need more kindness in our lives, we can begin by writing down how we can begin giving away the kindness we need most in our lives. If we need more happiness in our lives, we can begin by writing down ways in which we can make others happy. If understanding is what you seek from others, you can begin writing down how you can become a more understanding person, a more patient listener, a more compassionate friend.

When we begin writing down what kindnesses we need most in our lives, and how we can begin giving away this very thing, we will attract what we give away. Rodolfo Blanco, CRSH fourteen-year-old author, attests to this school of thought when he describes how an experienced sharing time with extended family members on a ski vacation resulted in family members spending more enjoyable times together during "regular" times back home.

In summary, the students at Coral Reef Senior High were asked to share some of their thoughts and feelings that project unusual deeds of kindness. Most of the resulting stories are drawn from their gratitude journals and are stories that awakened them to the basic truism that we do attract what we give away.

2. We Owe Much to the Kind Deeds of Others

When we engage in gratitude journal writing, we realize how much we owe to the kind actions of others. We are able to look back through the months and years and are amazed to realize the number of kind deeds that have been done for us. We realize that we all are interrelated, interconnected and interdependent. In like manner, we realize that all creation is interrelated, interconnected and interdependent.

Kind deeds have been done for us under various circumstances. Their spiritual values have been shown to us in the context of praise as well as blame, from unexpected persons. Experiences have shown us that every one of these acts of kindness has its root in the spirit of love.

It is frightening to think what we would have been had parents, relatives, friends, teachers, schoolmates, ministers been less kind to us. Realizing that we owe our wisdom of performing deeds of kindness to the wisdom of others makes us grateful. This feeling of sincere gratitude motivates us to gladly share beautiful stories about experiences of kindness so that others, too, can catch the spirit and perform deeds of kindness. In sharing these experiences we, too, feel the joy and lifelong commitment of helping to transform the world through deeds of kindness.

3. Developing a Kind Attitude

In seventeen-year-old Alicia Pantoja's story entitled *Gratitude,* she shares with us some important messages based on her personal experiences. Through gratitude journal writing, we come face to face with our true selves and are amazed at what we discover. "Know Thyself," are the famous words of Socrates that awaken us intellectually to the spiritual importance of self-awareness. We learn that attitude is everything, and consists basically of our thoughts and feelings. With this insight, we see it is necessary for us to develop a kind attitude. The messages contained in this volume teach us that we can develop a kind attitude by:

1. Practicing the elements of kindness, compassion and concern.
2. Placing the best interpretation on the behavior of others.
3. Avoiding the habit of passing judgment on others.
4. Resisting greed in all forms.
5. Controlling our inordinate feelings of anger.
6. Learning to bear others' offenses with kindness, compassion and concern.
7. Recognizing the consequences of unkind thoughts, feelings and actions.
8. Basing our thoughts, feelings and actions on kindness.

9. Discovering the transforming power of kindness.
10. Becoming a "candlelight" of kindness.

4. Learning to Think, Feel and Speak Kindly of Others

When we cultivate the art of speaking kindly to one another, we do not abuse the power of speech. We know that there is no greater source of friction than the one caused by the misuse of speech. The human tongue can be a very sharp and cutting instrument when powered by unkindnesses such as anger, pride, egotism, envy, greed, hatefulness, jealousy, revenge and all the forces that stem from fear.

We all have the capacity to be kind or cruel. At school, we are aware that it is always the disruptive behavior that receives the most attention. In gratitude journal writing, we want to highlight the kindnesses we see in our world, and we want to begin to let kind deeds receive the most attention.

According to the thoughts and feelings of our high school authors, the art of learning to think, feel and speak kindly is an attitude we can easily cultivate by:

(1) Seeing ourselves in others.
(2) Taking time to listen attentively to others.
(3) Avoiding making fun of others.
(4) Giving praise to others when it is earned.
(5) Forgiving others when they have been unkind to us.
(6) Apologizing when we have been unkind.
(7) Being kind to someone in need.
(8) Giving bear-hugs.
(9) Using kindness in correcting others
(10) Dedicating ourselves to Truth.

The wisdom from *Candlelights for the High School Student's World* tells us that children are permanently impressed by the loyalties of their adult associates, and that precept or even example is not lastingly influential. The children's stories tell us that growth is indicated by progress, and that real educational growth is indicated by increased appreciation of values such as love, joy, peace, patience, kindness, generosity, faithfulness, gentleness and self-control.

KINDNESS: THE ESSENCE OF LIFE

Kindness is more important than wisdom, and the recognition of this is the beginning of wisdom.
—Theodore Isaac Rubin

In summary, our young authors tell us that kindness is the heart and soul of love. Every kind deed is a step toward love—lovingkindness. It has been said that life is a learning institution in which you acquire knowledge regarding the means of making your life and the lives of your fellowmen happy. When we listen to the children, we find that education is founded in kindness.

As we listen to the child within us, we find that there is no power on earth that is so great as that of lovingkindness which never loses its strength, never knows its age and always renews itself.

Lovingkindness seeks to assert itself by deeds. Lovingkindness, a very real force, is not content with ordinary words. The effect of kindness is an eagerness to effectively perform, to effectively give service and to effectively console. If you do not wish to stop feeling the spirit of love, you must never cease to be kind.

Because kind thoughts inspire kind deeds, they are spiritual blessings. CRHS Student Government President, Edwina Bullard, awakens us to an awareness that a kind word spoken or an angry word withheld has produced love for many broken hearts. To have acquired the ability not to think or speak unkindly of others is a great accomplishment. Edwina makes it clear to us that the habit of placing the best interpretation on the conduct of others is one of the greatest acts of being kind. Greater than a kind thought, more refreshing than a kind word, is the union of thought and word in action.

In his book, *Confessions*, St. Augustine said, "We are what our works are. According as our works are good or bad, we are good or bad; for we are the trees, and our works are the fruit that one judges on the quality of the tree." These words of wisdom were exemplified in many of the young author's stories, especially that of seventeen-year-old Kristie Soares who is a published poet and an animal rights activist.

Kristie feels as one in the heart of all creation and believes that the universe wants our lives to be kindness in action because "Kindness imparts true wisdom."

In conclusion, this volume of our "Candlelights" series awakens us to thoughts and feelings of our young generation of dedicated leaders. They have revealed to us through human experiences that we can help transform the world through deeds of kindness. The following lyrics quoted from a 1966 edition of the *National Education Association Journal* beautifully sums up the message of wisdom given us by our young authors of *Candlelights for the High School Student's World*.

IT'S AMERICAN
It's American to be a kindly neighbor
It's American to lend a helping hand
To see that everyone in your community
Has an equal opportunity
To share the blessings of the land.

It's American to treat your neighbor kindly
Whatever his faith, race, nationality
So, think American! Act American!
Live American! Be American!
And we'll be one happy family.

INDEX

List of Young Authors and Titles of Their Stories

Candlelights for the High School Student's World
Co-Compiler

Ana Mederos-Blanco is a twenty-year veteran high school Theatre Arts teacher. A graduate of Miami-Dade Community College and Texas Women's University in Denton, Texas, she earned the Master's degree in Choreography and Directing for the Theatre and worked professionally in the theatre and dance fields for a while before falling in love with teaching and the students.

Ms. Mederos-Blanco has been awarded numerous honors during her teaching career, most notably the 2001 Presidential Scholar Teacher Recognition Award. She is listed in Who's Who Among America's High School Teachers, and she was a nominee for the Disney Teacher Award.

Ms. Mederos-Blanco and her husband Raymond are the proud parents of three sons, and she is delighted their sons love theatre as much as she does. She also is "thrilled to be working with Dr. Johnson on this incredible book!"

Candle Lights
FOR THE WORLD
Transforming the World Through Deeds of Kindness

Guidelines for Writing
"Candlelights" Stories
for the Book Series

GUIDELINES

Dear Friend of our Candlelights Series,

In the international war against terrorism, it is great, artistic writers like you who can help transform the world through spiritual stories of kindness from your personal world of kind thoughts, feelings and actions. We all love reading about human experiences that touch lives and lift spirits, and it is our hope that you have a myriad of inspirational stories to share for our Candlelights series to help spread love throughout the world.

1. The Three Components of an Acceptable "Candlelights" Story

(1) A "Candlelights" story is a true, inspirational story about people courageously performing deeds of **kindness** for another person. It is a dramatic and emotional story that touches lives and lifts spirits, and that covers the range of human emotions. It is an inter-denominational, spiritual and human work of art that helps the readers discover basic, simple strategies they can use in their own worlds to promote inner peace and experience abundant life...spiritually, physically and financially.

(2) A "Candlelights" story has a unique beginning, middle and ending that closes with a moral and powerful pizzazz. It is a personal story that comes from the depths of the heart, enabling the reader to feel more grateful, compassionate and loving; more enlightened, awakened and alive with the spirit of kindness.

(3) A "Candlelights" story awakens the reader to our

human interconnectedness, interrelatedness and interdependence, enabling her/him to joyfully feel as one in the heart of all creation.

2. Specific Guidelines for a "Candlelights" Story Portraying Kindness

(1) Writing deeply from the heart and portraying the human experience, tell a true story about a courageous deed of kindness that was performed by you or someone you know. Remember to stay focused on your subject of kindness because Kindness is love in action.

(2) With a passion, write your true story in a dramatic way that will trigger a myriad of spiritual thoughts, feelings and actions. Let your story have literary value. Include dialogue.

(3) Let your story (a) begin with a problem, situation or issue. In other words, put your protagonist high up in a tree and throw darts at him/her, (2) let the problem, situation or issue include thoughts, feelings and actions, and (3) let it end with a result, such as a lesson learned, a transformed life, or a spiritual surprise.

Because kindness encompasses all the virtues, you may focus on any one of the following nine virtues: (1) Love, (2) Joy, (3) Peace, (4) Patience, (5) Kindness, (6) Goodness, (7) Faithfulness, (8) Gentleness and (9) Self-Control. Remember, you may write more than one story.

3. A "Candlelights" Story is Not: An autobiography, a

eulogy, sermon, term paper, dissertation, personal testimony; a commentary on politics or controversial subjects.

4. How to Submit Your "Candlelights" Story

(1) Submit your story typed on plain white "8 1/2 X 11" paper, in 12-point Times New Roman font. Double spaced. 300-1200 words. Include a 25-50-word bio about you and/or about your latest book or project .

(2) We do not return submissions, so please do not send us your original copy.

(3) Unless you are writing for your assigned "Candlelights" series co-author of the book, you may submit your story to:

Mal-Jonal Productions, Inc.
Att: Alice W. Johnson, Ed.D.
Candlelights Series
16713 SW 107th Place
Miami, Florida, 33157-2965

5. About Your Published Story

Once we receive your story, we will mail you an acknowledgment card. If your story is published, you will be given a free copy of the book, and your name will be noted as author of the story. Proceeds from book sales will be awarded you through your specified organization, school, college or university department that solicited your story/stories and who will be the co-author of the book. Now is the time for you to be published and to help win the war against terrorism by sharing your stories of kindness to help transform the world. Kindness is the true, universal religion and your inherited divinity.

The Candlelights Series Editors
Mal-Jonal Productions, Inc., 16713 SW 107 Place,
Miami, FL 33157-2965
Tele: 305-253-4061 • Fax: 305-235-2600.
E-Mail: alicejohnsonmj@aol.com

Dear "Candlelights" Story Prospective Author,

The following are eleven "Candlelights" titles now underway for the first 9-set series. Each of the eleven (11) books will consist of nine chapters (the nine virtues of God) with approximately 2001 words in each chapter. Thus we have the " 9/11/2001" that unified us as a spiritual world on September 11, 2001, a date we shall always remember with deep compassion. Each of the books have professional co-authors with a passion for creatively "Writing for Him" and spreading love to help transform the world through kindness.

(1) Candlelights for the Family Caregiver's World
Candlelights for the Family Caregiver's World is the first volume in the series, and is the progenitor for the rest of the books. It is a very different book from the others because it is not a collection of stories. Rather, it is a book written by a family caregiver that focuses six spiritual keys of wisdom for avoiding caregiver-burnout and promoting inner peace. The book shows why family caregiving is a spiritual mission that teaches us the wisdom of kindness toward others. Thus, we learn from the experiences of family caregiving that our disabled loved ones are here to teach us **the wisdom of kindness.**

The following ten titles will be spinoffs of *Candlelights for the Family Caregiver's World* and compromise the first set of eleven books in the series. Each book will consist of a collection of ninety-nine (99) stories divided into nine sections. Each of the nine sections will represent the nine virtues with eleven stories in each section. The stories will be a memorial to the 9/11 experience, shining candlelights of kindness into the thoughts, feelings, and actions of humanity, transforming the world one story at a time. The moral of each *Candlelights* story is "Touching lives, Lifting Spirits"

(2) Candlelights for the High School Student's World
(3) Candlelights for the Middle School Student's World
(4) Candlelights for the Elementary School Student's World
(5) Candlelights for the Primary School Student's World
(6) Candlelights for the Kindergarten Student's World
(7) Candlelights for the Preschooler's World
(8) Candlelights for the Teacher's World
(9) Candlelights for the School Principal's World
(10) Candlelights for the Parent's World
(11) Candlelights for the Grandparent's World

Also projected are *Candlelights* collections that will portray other areas of the human experience focusing on the virtue of kindness. For example: *Candlelights for the Medical Student's World; Candlelights for the Clergyman's World; Candlelights for the College Student's World; Candlelights for the Mother's Spiritual World; Candlelights for the Spiritual Teenager's World; Candlelights for the Married Couple's World and Candlelights for the Religions of the World.*

LOVE IS A MYSTERY TO BE LIVED
(Excerpt from <u>Symbols of Love</u>)

by Alice and John Johnson

The tragedy of life is not death, but what we let die within us. Decide to feel the love within you; decide to feel happy, render others happy, proclaim your joy. Love passionately your miraculous life. Do not wait for a better world; be grateful for every moment of life. Switch on the positive buttons in yourself...those marked kindness, compassion, gratitude, optimism, serenity, confidence, positive thinking. Love, pray, meditate, and thank the Creator every day! Smile, laugh, whistle, sing, dance, look with fascination at everything and be aware that all creation is holy, even our adversities. Fill your lungs and heart with kindness, humility, freedom and gratitude. Unlock your inherited divinity and be yourself fully and immensely, realizing that God has given you unlimited possibilities. Take the labels off your mind and step boldly into your greatness. With a heart of humility, act like a king/queen and make your life a blessing to humanity until death. Feel God's love in your body, mind, heart and soul and be convinced of Eternal Life!

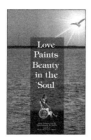  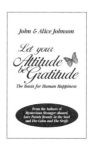
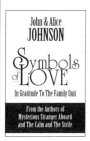 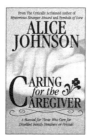  
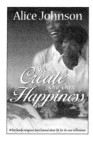  

ABOUT THE AUTHOR

ALICE JOHNSON is a writer/producer and a graduate of Savannah State University and Clark-Atlanta University. She and husband John, a Morehouse College and University of Cincinnati graduate who is a victim of multiple sclerosis, have written eleven books of inspiration, volumes of musical docudramas emphasizing multicultural education and literacy, and poetry portraying the human experience. The authors have been awarded numerous honors for their creative writings as caregiver and patient and their record is included in the 1999-2000 edition of *Marquis Who's Who in the South and Southwest*. Alice was honored with the *2000 Care Hero Award* presented by the national magazine *Today's Caregiver*.

ORDER FORM

BOOK TITLE	QTY.	BOOK TITLE	QTY.
~Mysterious Stranger Aboard	_____	~ We Create Our Own Happiness	_____
~Love Paints Beauty in the Soul	_____	~ Candlelights for the Family Caregiver's World	_____
~The Calm and The Strife	_____		
~Let Your Attitude be Gratitude	_____	~ Candlelights for the Middle School Student's World	_____
~Symbols of Love	_____		
~Caring for the Caregiver	_____	~ Candlelights for the High School Student's World	_____
~Love Finds Expression through kindness and Concern	_____		

$10.00 EACH OR $5.00 EACH FOR ORDERS OF 100 OR MORE!

Name _____

Address _____

City/State/Zip_____

Phone Number _____Fax Number _____

Make checks payable to Mal-Jonal Productions and mail to:
Mal-Jonal Productions, Inc.
16713 SW 107th Place • Miami, Florida 33157
www.maljonal.com